BROKEN TO BADASS

*Dealing with loss and pain
to recover quickly and
find your best self*

This book is dedicated to:

Taylor, Jasmine, Triniti, Ashton, Jasper – you are my reason for living.

Trin for being my comfort on the worst days

My mom who is the original badass woman

Joanna for being my rock at work

And to Myself, thank you for being such a badass.

Chapters

Prelude

Introduction

Broken chapters

1. Preparing for your trip through Hell

2. Your care team

3. Paradigm Shifts aka "The Stages of Grief"

4. When the tears come

5. Finding the will to live – dealing with suicidal thoughts

6. This is NOT your fault

Badass Chapters

1. Embracing The Experience – there is beauty in the pain

2. Fake it til you make it

3. Own your shit

4. The new love of your life

5. Get your badass outside

6. Revenge Life

Extra Chapter: Backsliding

bro·ken

'brōkən/

verb

1. **having been fractured or damaged and no longer in one piece or in working order.**

Smashed, shattered, fragmented, crushed

2. **(of a person) having given up all hope; despairing.**

"He went to his grave a broken man"

Defeated, beaten, subdued

Prelude:

I wrote this book because I survived a living hell and I would not wish that pain on anyone. I had no manual or survival guide to help me. I had to wing it. I got clichéd advice from books and people. I also, got very helpful advice from books and people. But nobody or nothing could prepare me for what I was really going to experience. I had no idea how excruciatingly painful it would be and I had no idea if I would survive it or if it would ever end.

If you are in it right now you need to know three things:

1. This is going to be one of the most painful things you will probably ever experience

2. It will end eventually, but not anytime soon.

3. You will survive it and you can use the power of it to have a better life in the end.

This book is yours to use however you want, whenever you want. You can start at the beginning and read it straight through or you can read whichever chapter you need when you need it the most. It is divided into two parts; Broken chapters for the hard times and Badass chapters for when it's time to get the fuck up and be strong again. It is not one of those books where the author draws out each chapter by repeating themselves or adding in a bunch of bullshit. It's short so you can just read it, and use it.

This is also not an all-encompassing book of tragedy. Every person who reads it will have their own challenges and paths they have to take. You might have kids, you may not, you may have been cheated on, physically abused …the list goes on. I am not going to try to pretend to know your individual path. I am writing it to hopefully help ease some of your pain and shorten that path, that right now seems never ending.

This book can be thrown as hard as you want, it can be hugged. You can sleep with it next to you so you can open it up at 2a. when you can't sleep and read the portion on meditation in the Baddassery Daily chapter or just read the words:

ITS NOT YOUR FAULT.

YOU ARE WORTHY.

THIS WON'T LAST FOREVER

For the sake of reading this book, I use the word Her as my ex's name, or She. When you see these capitalized, I am speaking directly about Her. I changed her name because it was a "Trigger" for me. "Triggers" are the things that bring memories and pain. I will explain in more detail in Chapter 1. I included stories from men and women who have gone through break-ups as well as an interview I did with a divorce attorney because hearing other the stories from other people helped me, maybe one of their stories will speak to you.

You are beginning what will come to be one of the most challenging times of your life.

You have a choice…you can let it break you…or you can let it build you.

The choice will be yours every hour of every day for a while, and you will consistently need to make that choice. The good news is, if you choose wrong sometimes, there is always a new minute, new hour and new day. New opportunities to be strong constantly present themselves.

This process has no definite timeline, it could take a weeks, months or years. Hopefully I can help you to expedite the process and find your happiness again. When I was going through it I had spoken to so many people about their experiences and the time frame varied widely for healing. I told myself, there is no fucking way I am letting myself feel like this for 6 months, a year, 3 years. I embraced the experience and fully went through it while working on myself and I was over the pain in five months. I know five months seems long, but believe me I had to put in work to recover this quickly.

You can and will be better every day.
You will be stronger every day and one day....
Someday.... You will be badass again.

Broken

"Let me tell you something you already know. The world ain't all sunshine and rainbows. It's a very mean and nasty place and I don't care how tough you are, it will beat you to your knees and keep you there permanently if you let it. You, Me, or nobody is gonna hit as hard as life. But it ain't about how hard you hit. It's about hard you can get hit and keep moving forward. How much you can take and keep moving forward. That's how winning is done" Rocky

I had the perfect life. Perfect. I have that backstory of strength and perseverance that got me from being a kid who used to dumpster dive for toys to the only college educated person in my entire family. I survived an abusive relationship, single motherhood to three daughters while working three jobs AND going to college. Then coming out late in life. I gave my kids what I like to call a "Norman Rockwell" kind of childhood where they lived a life that books are written about. They turned out to be kick ass, smart, beautiful, independent women. Then I married the most perfect human I had ever met. She was my best friend, my partner, my confidant, my sexual fantasy, the girl of my dreams. I called Her my "perfect" and "My everything." We had 8 years of complete bliss. We never fought. We laughed, we loved, our sex life remained awesome.

Then one day….it was over. For no reason and no notice.

I met my wife in my senior year of college. We were both seniors in the same major and had quite a few classes together. The first time I looked in her eyes I thought she was the most beautiful human I had ever seen. I was 34 and she was only 21. I was a lesbian, she was straight, and we were both in relationships. Her, with an older guy for 3 years. Me with a feisty girl for the past 3 years. The first time we spoke was in the computer lab when she asked me if I had a Myspace. She added me that day and I commented on one of her photos of how beautiful she was. The next day I sat next to her and looked at her eye to eye for the first time, she was the most beautiful human I had ever seen. She broke up with her boyfriend by that Friday and I broke up with my girlfriend. The first time we ever kissed I knew this was different, it was powerful and perfect. The first time we ever held hands we both knew it was forever. Not only was she my dream girl, she was instantly my best friend. We got married the first time a year later, signed domestic partnership papers. Then we officially got married twice over years later, once a fairytale outdoor wedding and once at city hall in San Francisco the year it became legal. I asked her to marry me every day of our lives and she always said yes. I would ask her every day to love me forever, and every day she would reply "I am actively loving you forever."

We had the best relationship. We never fought, we didn't even bicker. You know those little fights couples get in about toothpaste, toilet paper….laundry…we didn't even have those because in my mind everything she did was perfect. She was a nerd at heart and her dorky ways were the cutest thing I had ever seen. We would cook together, clean together, workout together and always be on the same page. We could never get enough of each other. She was the most attractive human I had ever laid eyes on and I couldn't keep my eyes or hands off her. We went through life hand in hand, and like magnets we refused to be apart. Everyone that knew us wanted we had.
We were the unattainable perfection of true love.

We had it all even beyond the two of us. We had a picture perfect family, traveled constantly, and the family played and laughed and broke out in random song all the time. We had three daughters, adopted twin boys, a bonus son, 2 dogs and a cat. We had a big, loud, crazy, happy, dream family that outsiders were drawn to because of the sheer love and positivity. We lived in San Francisco, Scottsdale and we even randomly sold everything and moved to Maui with the family and lived there for 9 months. Playing, hanging out, enjoying the sun. It was a dream life.

It was right after Maui when it happened. I got a request from my company to move back to Arizona. I didn't want to go, it's funny, I just had a bad feeling about leaving. Our dream had always been to find a way to be together all day and we had accomplished that in Maui. We were both working remotely, so we worked two feet from each other and I could go over and kiss her beautiful face all day long as much as I wanted. It was a dream come true. When the conversation arose I expressed my concerns about giving up that life but she pushed me to go because she wanted the best for me and also it happened to coincide with the time when the kids were all hitting the adult years and moving back to Arizona to go to college. She knew I would want to keep the family together, she pushed and we moved back to Arizona. We moved into an apartment since all the kids, except one, simultaneously moved out and took the pets with them. We had sold everything we owned so the apartment only had a bed, a rug and 2 chairs. It was empty. This was a really hard transition, losing all of the family out of the house, the pets and living without the warmth and familiarity we were used to.

A month after we got back She got a call from her childhood friend who had just broken up with his longtime girlfriend. She ended up going back home to support him and help him move out, just like a real friend should. I was in St. Louis for work and she was back in our home town. We were texting constantly like we always did when we were apart. It was a Saturday and she had been texting me that she should not have left, she hated it there, she missed me so much. Then the texts stopped Saturday night. I kept texting her asking her what she was up to and to send me pictures. She sent me a photo of a girl I used to date, whom she had always been jealous of, they were at a bar and the caption read "here is a fucking picture." I am so naïve that I did not think of anything of it.

She was only gone for four days but when she got home she was a different person. She was strangely cold and removed and the colder she was the more I freaked out. I started pushing her to see where her head was. I turned into someone I don't even recognize. In all of our years together I have never yelled, been mean, or done anything crazy. However, I knew something was happening and I turned into a crazy person. I started pushing her to make decisions and the more I pushed the colder she was…the colder she was… the more I lost it.

We had a huge fight, our first big fight in the entire relationship and then it was over. It happened on a Sunday and She was gone on a flight to California by noon while I was laying on the floor dying. The pain was so intense; it was squeezing me from my very soul out to my skin. There was no reason, other than the ONE fight that ONE day.

Nothing had changed between us and yet my forever girl was gone….forever.

There was no lead up, no signs, no "closure." She was here and then she was gone and it was like a death. I went from having a big house full of love to an empty apartment that was like a tomb.

That day was the last day I would ever see her again. It was... in a sense....a death.

I would find out a few months later that the girl she was dating and living with the girl she had sent me a photo of.

Like the end of a beautiful dream....it was over and there was nothing I could do to get it back.
The next month would forever redefine who I was and what I was capable of.

I am a strong person in every sense of the word. I never give up, I push for what I want and get it. I have always known that the only limits that exist are within your own mind. I know these things. And yet, I was not myself anymore. In that month I spoke to three counselors, an attorney who was like a counselor, dozens of friends. I read 5 books on healing, dealing with grief etc.. I did yoga, ran, meditated.

It sounds so strong and healthy, right?

I also sat in a bathtub holding a razorblade, stood at the edge of the sidewalk as cars whizzed past and thought how simple it would be to step out. I sat on the ledge of a building and imagined closing my eyes and falling into relief. I would go from hope to hate, then pain, then nothing. I didn't eat, I didn't sleep. I texted her 200 times in one night and a thousand times that month, hoping for answers, signs, closure, anything. I was broken and confused and it was only through strength, the love of family and friends and dedication to survival that I came out on the other side of hell.

Chapter 1

Preparing for your trip through Hell.

Fire runs through my body with the pain of loving you. Pain runs through my body with the fires of my love for you. Sickness wanders my body with my love for you. Pain like a boil about to burst with my love for you. Consumed by the fire with my love for you. I remember what you said to me. I am thinking of your love for me. I am torn by your love for me. Pain and more pain. Where are you going with my love? I am told you will go from here. I am told you will leave me here. My body is numb with grief. Remember what I have said, my love. Good bye, my love, good bye.

This poem, recited by an anonymous Kwakuitl Indian of Southern Alaska to a missionary in 1896

Hell exists on earth. If you are in it now…BREATHE. Seriously. In the first few days I couldn't even breathe, it was so painful when the flood of tears and wailing coming from deep inside my soul. You have to remind yourself to breathe. The pain you are experiencing is very real and it is here to stay… for now. You have experienced a shock to your system and your biological responses are trying to protect you during this time of trauma. It is trauma, so it's not only okay to cry but you need to allow yourself to feel the emotions and be raw.

 The second the car pulled away with my love in it, I collapsed onto the living room rug, grabbed onto the fibers with my fingers, face down as I sobbed uncontrollably. I held onto the rug like it was the only thing keeping me from sliding off the earth. This wasn't ordinary crying. This was in one word, excruciating. The pain was absolutely unreal. I felt like my insides were being ripped out. My stomach cramped as I writhed in pain, then I would vomit from tears and pain. I would cry all day for days and feel absolutely exhausted and yet I couldn't sleep. At night I would finally fall asleep and then an hour later I would wake up from my heart beating so fast I thought I was having a heart attack. Then I would instantly start crying again and just hold the pillow. Anxiety and insomnia. Not fucking fun. How this shit doesn't kill you is beyond me.

You will ask yourself:

"Why?" "What did I do to deserve this" "What do I do now?" "When will the pain stop?" "Why does this hurt so bad" "How do I breathe again?" "Why don't they love me?"

WHY? WHY? WHY?

So go ahead and CRY. Let it out. A change has happened and you have no answers. You will ask yourself these questions a million times and you will go through a range of emotions in the next few hours, days, weeks and maybe months. But regardless of how you feel right now...

YOU WILL BE OKAY AGAIN.

I hated when people would say that to me. "You will be okay again Shianne" I always responded with a simple polite "Thank you" or "I know" but I wanted to scream:

"YOU DON'T KNOW THAT!! SHE WAS MY EVERYTHING. I WILL NEVER BE OKAY AGAIN"

They were right though. I really was going to better than okay one day, I would be badass.

You too will be better than okay; you will be badass. After all, the best revenge for the bullshit that life throws our way is to take it, handle it and throw it back in life's face with the strength of a thousand men.

First, you need to prepare yourself for the journey you are about partake in. Imagine the Lord of The Rings and you are the Hobbit, it is going to be a journey of epic proportions and you are going to battle some horrible demons. This shit is real and it is going to be super fucked up and you'll wonder of it is even worth it, but if you are prepared you can overcome the challenges and throw that damn ring into the fire where it belongs. Literally.

FIRST STEPS:
Things to ELIMINATE or REFRAIN from RIGHT NOW

There are things that will give you instant satisfaction, gratification or even a short lived burst of relief but may have devastating long term or negative residual effects. If you want to get through this faster I strongly recommend NOT doing these things.

1. DROP THE PHONE AND STOP ALL CONTACT.

This will be the hardest thing I tell you to do…but it is CRUCIAL. Immediately stop texting the person who left you. STOOOPPP. Nope stop. Nope. There is no good reason. Take it from me. It feels good at the time and you will rationalize your behavior with "I just need to say this one thing" "Maybe they don't understand why I …" "Oh this one is good, they need to know" EVERYONE told me I needed to stop contacting her and it was physically impossible for me to stop. It was my only connection to her and I would just text her everything that came in my mind. NON STOP.

One night I text her 200 times. With no response. The next morning she text back *"WTF. I went to bed early. I wasn't ignoring you. I woke up to 200 texts"* Opps. Even the lawyer I talked to said the one thing he knew for sure in his 26 years of practicing divorce law is that you cannot contact the other person, they have to feel your absence if there is even the slightest chance they will come back.

For two weeks I text her nonstop and never got much more than 2-3 words. Until finally when I went to Oregon for 4 days to be with my friend Carmen. Carmen took my phone so that

I could not text Her. In those four days I thought that I had grown so much and had come so far in my healing. Then on the fourth day while I am sitting at the airport I get this text:

"I'm not gone and I don't want to be cut out of your life"

What kind of bullshit text is that? I should NOT have responded to it but it gave me a taste of hope and I asked so I text back and asked what it meant, 4 days went by again before I heard from her and I had taken 3 steps back in my growth and was sad all over again.

Give your phone to someone. DO IT RIGHT NOW. And turn off social media. DO NOT post about your relationship. I am a business woman, not a teenager and yet I posted on Facebook that I was "Walking through hell." It was a plea for help, I think I wanted someone anyone to take my side, to comfort me. But it didn't do me any good and it won't for you either. It will embarrass you later and it makes you look like the crazy one. Turn social media off, get away from your phone. Trust me, you will thank me later.

IT'S LIKE FUCKING HEROINE. I am not a crazy person but if you were to have read my texts…you would not be reading this book because you would think I was insane. I begged her for 7 weeks straight! SEVEN! When I look back at my own texts, I am embarrassed.

This is an addiction and it gives you instant release but it is only seconds of relief, then it turns into grief and desperation. The more you text, the more despair.

Because let me tell you something:

THEY WILL NEVER SAY WHAT YOU WANT THEM TO SAY

THEY WILL NEVER SAY WHAT YOU NEED THEM TO SAY

IF THEY WANTED TO BE WITH YOU THEY WOULD

THERE IS NO SUCH THING AS CLOSURE

This might not even be about you. This might be about them. I was so wrapped up in our love, our relationship, it was perfect…why would she leave…what had I done? Why didn't she love me?

Now that I can see clearly, it had nothing to do with me, or us. As much as we would like to believe that when we are a couple, we are one soul…we aren't. They are an individual and individuals have needs, wants and issues that we know nothing about and a lot of times can't fix or help them with. They have to sort their thoughts, solve their own problems and come to their own conclusions. If you keep interfering with that path they will never find what they are looking for and they will never realize they love or want you. They may not ever realize that anyway but if you are constantly contacting them…they definitely won't.

Your best chance at saving your relationship is NO CONTACT.

Your best chance at saving yourself is NO CONTACT.

In Pema Chodron's book *When Things fall Apart*, she says in regard to addictions "So many times we have indulged in the short term pleasure of addiction. We've done it so many times that we know that grasping at this hope is a source of misery that makes a short-term pleasure a long-term hell."

This is addiction and you need to go cold turkey, that short term pleasure is lengthening your path through hell.

2. Eliminate triggers

Have someone sweep your house for anything they can see that will trigger you. Take pictures down, bag their stuff up, get rid of toiletries in the bathroom. I even got rid of her coffee cups, favorite water bottle. Books, their pillow. You name it, if it was "theirs" it needs to go for now. Yes, it is going to be a painful process. You are already in fucking pain I know, but if you don't do this it will only make things worse later. Have someone bag it all up and put it somewhere where you won't see it…or burn it. Just kidding don't burn it, you'll regret that later. Or…burn it…I don't give a fuck.

I even changed her name to "Her" in my phone and deleted her ID photo because they were triggers. It was horrible every time I looked at my phone to see "My Love" with her beautiful face looking at me. Like the fucking devil. I deleted Her off Facebook because I would stare at it a million times a day waiting for some sign. I thought I could see her doing something that would explain what happened. I would close it and open it, close it and open it. Check again and again. It kept me in a state of desperation and craziness. Eliminating triggers will be hard at first because it is going to make it feel very real and probably increase the pain. You'll look and see where pictures were or where their clothes were. Arrange things so it doesn't look like anything is missing. Get new bedding if you want. Get photos to replace the photos on the wall. It's like ripping off a band-aid. if you leave the triggers up, you will continually be taking backward steps. If you truly want to heal faster, get rid of the triggers.

Also, it is not necessary to tell them, nor is it necessary to give them their stuff or find reasons to contact them. Which you will. There will be so many "reasons" but DO NOT CONTACT THEM. If you need to give them their stuff, have a friend do it for you.

I knew in the early days of this hell that she would only talk to me about finances, her stuff etc… So I would find things to make her talk to me about. I had the boxes of her stuff and I obsessed over how I would get her to react. I went from "I am throwing everything away" to "If you want it, come face me." Then I finally just let go and carefully and considerately boxed it up and had a friend who was traveling to California drop it off. In the end you have to make sure you handle it in a way that won't make you feel bad about yourself or give you any regrets. I am not saying this for them, or because it's the right thing to do or any of that bullshit. Fuck them. I am worried about you. I want to protect you so that when all is said and done you can hold your head up, rise above and walk into your revenge life with no regrets.

Now be strong and have a friend get rid of their shit for you.

3. People to avoid

If you know anyone who is negative, you cannot be around them right now. Also, someone else going through a breakup cannot help you and the two of you will only bring each other down. One of my best friends and her boyfriend broke up a week before we did and she was in a bad place. We text a couple times one day and then we stayed away from each other for 6 months. It was not because we don't love each other, but because the blind cannot and should not lead the blind. It may feel good to have someone who "understands" and you can bitch together but it won't get either of you anywhere. The reality is that you'll both just wallow in hell and misery together.

Anyone who tells you that you are "over reacting" or undermines your actual feelings should not be in your life right now. They aren't helpful and they will actually make you turn your sadness toward your own self-worth, which can have detrimental effects. You need positive, helpful people who are willing to listen and not judge you. The best person I had was my dear friend/brother Liam. We had been friends for over 10 years and he knew both of us very well. He gave me insight from both sides but never passed judgment and never said anything negative about Her. He was the best human to go through this with, period. (I will rent him out for a fee)

Lastly, anyone who tries to get you to drink or do drugs. They aren't your friend and those things will only cause you more pain in the long run.

Assess your friend and family group and make the right choices as to who you surround yourself with because your badass self cannot happen without positive reinforcement.

4. Drugs & alcohol

I drink maybe 3-4 times a year. I don't smoke, and I don't do drugs. She left me on Sunday. I had the bright idea of going out the following Friday. I drank. I did drugs for the first time in many, many years. It felt fun, I laughed and had a great time. I felt like myself, I wasn't sad or hurting. I had my friends and I was out and it was great.

The next day however, I was back in my deep sadness and it took me 3 days to recover my footing. I had worked so hard to stop crying incessantly, to be able to function and breathe. Now I was back at square one.

Also, in the first days when I couldn't sleep for days, I was exhausted and I got a bright idea. I took 3 sleeping pills and drank 3 shots of vodka and STILL ONLY SLEPT FOR TWO HOURS. I woke up and took 3 more sleeping pills and slept for another 2 hours. It was fucking horrible. I even text Her that I had taken sleeping pills and was drinking to get a response...all I got was "Stop. Don't do that." (We will discuss suicidal thoughts more later).

Drugs and alcohol only prolong the healing. If you want to stop hurting, you need to allow yourself to FEEL it first.

Alcohol and drugs numb it but it's like a dam. The water just builds up on the other side and it is eventually going to flood over you.

Drugs and Alcohol WILL NOT STOP inevitable impending pain, THEY ONLY DELAY AND INTENSIFY IT.

Face this bullshit head on, don't medicate.

5. Sad music, TV, Movies

On my way to Oregon I was sitting at the airport and I put my earphones in and turned on a song that reminded me of Her. Up to this point I was doing fairly well, had been journaling, functioning and crying way less. The weight on my chest was bearable. Then the fucking music. I started writing at the airport as the music played...a deep sadness came over me and tears were streaming down my cheeks as I wrote. I was falling into a dark hole of emotion with every song that played. Then "Gravity" by Sara Bareilles came on.

Something always brings me back to you

It never takes too long

No matter what I say or do

I'll still feel you here 'till the moment I'm gone

You hold me without touch

You keep me without chains

I never wanted anything so much than to drown in your love

And not feel your reign

Set me free, leave me be

I don't want to fall another moment into your gravity

Here I am, and I stand

So tall, just the way I'm supposed to be

But you're on to me and all over me

Oh, you loved me 'cause I'm fragile

When I thought that I was strong

But you touch me for a little while

And all my fragile strength is gone

Set me free, leave me be

I don't want to fall another moment into your gravity.....

I replayed it over and over for the 2.5 hour flight. By the time I landed I was an empty shell. Just pathetic, desperate and in pain. It was almost as bad as my night out.

Here is my journal entry, verbatim, from the day before the airport fiasco:

Your only goal =

Make yourself feel good and do whatever you need to do to give yourself confidence to get through the day.

Be grateful

I am grateful for the intense beauty in the situation. It is horrible yes, but it is beautiful in the change it is creating within me.

Enjoy the process.

The time to enjoy myself is in the now.

Here is my journal entries while listening to sad music like an idiot:

Life goes on…for her like its nothing. Meanwhile for me it hurts to breathe. She smiles and laughs and forgets all about me. Nothing can take her out of my mind. I feel so alone. I know I have to let her go but how? She is the ledge and I *holding on for life. If I let go I feel like I will fall to my death. I hurt constantly.*

A BIG DIFFERENCE between the two. Put the sad music down and back away. I will say there was a pretty angry alternative rock song that came on about getting over an ex and that one felt pretty good because I started singing/ shouting for her to fuck herself. It's probably not healthy to go to the other extreme either.

Like drugs and alcohol, these things may feel good at the time but they bring you down and they will keep you down. You'll go through numb stages where you feel lost and confused so you may even put something sad on to bring the tears back because the lost feeling can be even worse at times. Same goes for TV, Movies etc...DON'T DO IT. Find something healthy instead.

THINGS TO DO and SUPPLIES:

1. Water.

You will dehydrate yourself from crying. Also, because your body is in shock you don't want to eat and then you don't really want to drink. Treat it like a sickness. Keep a bottle of water next to your bed and remind yourself to drink every 30 minutes or so. Water will help you heal faster and keep your body healthy.

2. Healthy food.

You aren't hungry most likely. All the tears going down into your stomach make you sick and most of the time you won't feel hungry. Best diet ever, just think of how good you'll look! I could not eat for days. Then barely ate for weeks. I lost 17lbs in the first couple of weeks, not healthy but I had always been the exact right weight until I met her...she loved to eat...so I learned to cook really well. The weight loss was one step in becoming myself again and it was the silver lining to my hell.
 If you do want to eat or tend to eat your feelings, stay away from rich, fatty, greasy foods. While you are going through this if you ingest anything that is hard for your body to digest it will actually take a toll on your system. Eat foods that you

eat when you have the flu and the BRAT diet (Banana, rice, applesauce, toast). They are easy to digest and much less likely to make you throw up when you cry. Also, limit your over eating! When the dust settles and you finally lift your head up you don't to go through the regret of weight gain.

3. A quiet, warm place.

Most likely your bedroom, unless your bedroom is too much to bear in terms of memories. Then stay in a spare room or pop up a tent in the living room and create your space. Get your favorite blankets, some soft pillows and anything that makes you happy but doesn't remind you of them. You are healing and you need a warm, safe place to do it in. Take care of all the details of what makes you happy. I changed all of my bedding but kept my pillows. I put a new candle in the room that didn't smell like anything I was accustomed to. I took away every single thing of Hers and cleaned the room from top to bottom. I made it MY space. You need YOUR space to feel safe. Put happy photos up, pictures of you and friends or family. Find old pictures of you before you knew THEM and when you were happy. They will remind you that you were happy before you met them and you can be happy again.

4. A new journal

This is crucial. You will be using it every day for a while. You need to write out what is happening. It helps you move forward, it helps sort your thoughts and it helps reflect on what the real truth is. It needs to be a brand new one. I started to use an old one and the first two pages were writings from Her about epic dates we had. I read them every time I opened the journal and it would open all my wounds again. I even sent her pictures of what she had written, hoping she would see it and come to her senses and run back to me. I shake my head at myself.

Start fresh. Sometimes you will just ramble on and on and sometimes you'll write things that come from deep inside that you didn't know existed.

DISCLAIMER: Regardless of what you write, it does not mean it is all true.

As you will discover in the next chapter you will go through several paradigm shifts in short periods and those will be reflected in your writing. You may write things that feel true but are just amplified by your intense emotional state. I look back at what I wrote and I laugh at how crazy I was and how delusional. They don't have to be true, write whatever you need to write and then let it go. The journal will go with you everywhere and be an outlet for the roller coaster of emotions you will experience.

It will also help you to NOT CONTACT them. Instead of texting, emailing and calling Them...write it in your journal. Use it as an outlet. Pretend you are speaking to them if you need to. You may think about getting a new journal after significant stages so that you can start fresh. After I finally let Her go, I started a new journal that was all about me...not Her.

5. Books

There is nothing that you are experiencing that someone else hasn't gone through, even if it feels like no one could ever know. There are great books out there that will help you get through this, give you a new perspective or help you reflect on what is happening for the better. I read 5 books in 4 weeks. A couple didn't really do much for me. But "When things fall apart" by Pema Chodron helped me recover much faster in the darkest days, not be a salesperson here but you should seriously order it right now. I also read "Succulent Wild Woman" By Sark a great book for regaining your love for yourself, and "Option B" by Sheryl Sandberg. Sandberg's is about the death of her husband and even though my wife had not died I could relate to everything she went through. It helped me understand the severity of the emotions I was experiencing, but when I was about ¾ of the way through I realized it was actually just making me feel worse because I was also feeling Sheryl's pain. It is such a beautiful horrific story of love and lost that I kept crying with her sorrow and I found myself wallowing in my own suffering.

Be cognizant of how things effect you, something that helped me may not help you and vice versa but be aware and always go with things that have a positive effect. The sad books help in the beginning when you need to understand that what you are feeling is natural, then staying with positive books help once you are past the darkest days.

Pick books that speak to you and highlight your favorite phrases or themes so you can refer back to them, and pick books that help YOU be a better YOU. Don't always focus on the breakup. Maybe career books, fiction (NOT ROMANCE). I highly recommend the entire Harry Potter series. No I am not a nerd. Okay fine, a little.

I read *Eat Pray Love* by Elizabeth Gilbert in month 5 and although the movie was good, the book was SO much better. I identified with the author and she wrote how I felt, it really helped me feel like I wasn't alone and it gave me a new perspective on a possible future.

6. Download a meditation APP.

I have heard some people say when they went through this, all they did was sleep. I envy those people. I would have done anything to sleep. I slept roughly 4.5 hours the first 5 days. Which intensified my craziness and my lack of strength to combat the paradigm shifts. I would bounce all over the place in my mind and I wished I could have taken a drill to my temple to get rid of the psychotic roller coaster of uncontrollable thoughts. Then my friend told me about this meditation app called "Insight." And it changed everything for me. I laid in bed at 10p. with my arms at my sides like a corpse and made myself as comfortable as possible. I turned on one of the top rated sleep meditations and that night I didn't wake up until 2a. I had slept from 10p-2a!!! Four hours may not seem like a lot but it was more than I had gotten in the past 5 days. I woke up and my heart was beating and I did my usual cycle of crying so hard I almost puked, until the tears were gone. Got up blew my nose and then laid down and put the meditation back on. It worked again! I slept from 3:30 to 6a. I kept repeating this cycle over the next few days and the time I slept grew longer and longer. I even used it for naps on the hardest days. Then I started using the morning meditations to start my day with the right mindset. It was a life saver. Literally.

7. Surround yourself with family and friends. (THE MOST IMPORTANT THING)

Friends. Relatives. You need to talk and they need to listen if they love you. I interviewed so many people for this book and the one common thing that helped every single one of them was friends and family.

I WOULD NOT HAVE SURVIVED THIS WITHOUT MY FAMILY. PERIOD.

I am lucky enough to have the best kids on the planet, the coolest brother and the most wonderful supportive mom. They saved my life.

I will go through this in greater detail in the "Care Team" chapter but for now you need someone who can remove your triggers, get your supplies, talk you down from the ledge. Someone who is not negative! The person that comes over and says "you are better off without them, they are an asshole. Move on" this does not help.

The WORST cliché statement ever is "Everything happens for a reason" I want to punch this well-meaning person right in their kind face. You will find yourself saying "ya" but really you automatically take the opposing stance in your head. The person you want is the one that knows you well enough to tell you the truth and that is positive but not a ray of fucking sunshine. A good listener.

This list isn't all inclusive and everyone is different, but keeping all the positive around you and all the negative away is crucial. Some of these things will feel really good instantly but will lengthen your healing process, elongate the pain and in many cases make things worse. Keep people around you who make you laugh, the funny sarcastic people are the best. My kids are hilarious and we would laugh through the tears, we would laugh at how stupid it all was, we would laugh at the fact that it was Her loss and we still had an awesome family.

Speaking of friends and family…In order to eliminate everything and get everything you need, ask someone else take care of getting this done for you. Your job right now is to take care of yourself. Imagine if someone you loved was very ill and hurt, how would you want then to be treated? You need to treat yourself in that manner. In the coming days you cannot be there for anyone else, you need to take care of you. If you have children, get someone to help you with them. Just for the first few days.

Together we are going to go through this journey and all of its pain. What you are going through is horrible, no doubt. But it can be a beautiful, life changing experience that catapults you into the change you have been needing to find yourself, love yourself, and have a better life.

Because you can and you will.

Summary

ELIMINATE:

1. THE PHONE AND STOP ALL CONTACT.

2. Triggers

3. Negative people

4. Drugs & alcohol

5. Sad music, TV, Movies

GO GET:

1. Water.
2. Healthy food.
3. A quiet, warm place.

4. A new journal

5. Books

6. Download a meditation APP.

7. SURROUND YOURSELF WITH FAMILY AND FRIENDS

YOU CAN DO THIS AND YOU WILL MAKE IT THROUGH!

CHAPTER 2

Your Care Team

A broken heart is the worst, it's like having broken ribs. Nobody can see it but the pain is unbearable every time you breathe. - Author unknown

Chapter 2: Your care team

Family

I had my kids. My beautiful, perfect, amazing kids. The girls were hurt and devastated because when She left me, she left them and cut all contact with them. She was the only other parent they had ever known and they deeply loved her, and she was just gone forever without even a goodbye. The day she left she was leaving to the airport four hours early and the kids were trying to get to the house but she wouldn't even wait to say goodbye.

Taylor my oldest daughter, 22, had been planning on giving Her official "adoption" papers for Mother's day, which would have been a month after She left. Taylor was always more guarded and reserved because she was secretly the most sensitive one and was afraid of being hurt. She had come into Taylor's life when Tay was 13-years-old. Taylor had resisted Her for years because Taylor had been old enough to know the hurt from her father, so she was very guarded about letting anyone in. Despite her trepidation she eventually she grew to love Her deeply. The day this all happened, Tay was logical and level headed as usual but every time she would try to talk her chin would quiver. After all Taylor's resisting, the one thing that she always feared happened…she was abandoned. She said to me one day by the pool, in her cool calm demeanor… "I have just come to realize we aren't worthy of having a second parent I guess." My heart almost fell out of my chest.

Jasmine is the middle daughter, 19, and was the closest with Her since they day they met. We would always say that if one of the girls was biologically Her's it would be Jasmine. They were best friends and Jasmine did everything to make Her proud, including playing football just like She had done years before. When She left she didn't even really say goodbye and she didn't reach out to the girls for over a month. Jasmine was devastated. She almost quit school because she said it was the one thing her that She had valued and now Jas didn't care about it anymore because she was doing it to make Her proud.

Triniti is the youngest, 16, and had recently gone through a bad break up of her own. She had been in a relationship with one boy for the past 3 years and it ended abruptly. First love. She went through her own hell and could have really used this book. Trin was numb to everything and had the toughest exterior but I knew she was deeply hurt by Her actions. It finally surfaced one day when she collapsed into my arms and just let the tears flow.

We all kept our distance from each other for the first week; I think because I wasn't in a place to help them because I couldn't even help myself, but also they were going through their own emotional journeys.

After the first week the girls all came over for the first time and we laid in a pile on that same rug and just cried and held each other. We talked about our feelings and how hurt we all were. The themes were repetitive "It's surreal" "I can't believe this happened" "I thought we were so happy" "Why would she leave?" All of the million dollar questions that will never be answered, but we all felt the same. We had our own support group.

The boys were surprisingly supportive. Ashton, one of my 18-year-old twins, would come over and hug me and say "I'm sorry mama" and I would cry and talk and he would just say "It's going to be hard." He didn't know what else to say and yet it was the exact right thing. My other boy Jasper, Ashton's brother, is much more affectionate and would just hug me. Those hugs were solid gold and I just needed that affection. The boys had only been in our lives a few years and although they were hurt, they were handling it well. It was weeks later that I found out that were taking it hard. We had given them a stable home and family, something they had never had before and it all crashed down and shattered their new found security.

The kids ended up being what would save me in the long run. First, because I couldn't kill myself because of what it would do to them. Second, because they needed me to set a standard for how to deal with hard times and third because when I saw how she had hurt them it gave me the twinge of anger I needed to pull myself up and make an oath that I was going to survive and she was not going to break me or my family. My family needed me, so does yours. We have to be strong for the people we love because they hurt too.

My brother from another mother, Liam, was absolutely crucial to my seeing things in a normal balanced way. He knew both of us very well and was close to both of us. He gave me perspective and could speak to my skewed perspective. He gave me insight into things I hadn't seen, without being judgmental or negative. Liam was also a life saver because he was the only one I really divulged my overwhelming desire to end my life to. He was there every single time I needed him and would drop everything to be by my side. They don't make people like Liam anymore.

Finally, my mom. She is the most positive, happy, generous human you could ever meet. She loves everyone, even strangers. She lives in California but I would call her and cry and vent and she would say "I know baby" and just let me cry for hours. She didn't give me any advice or any clichés, simply support and love. My poor mom had loved my wife so deeply that she too was angry and so heartbroken. She went through her own grieving process because she had lost a daughter-in-law. (I used to joke that my mom loved Her more than me, but not now! Ha.)

The entire family was hurt and injured and we each had to go through our own process of healing and everyone handled it differently. Fortunately, they all held me up until I could be strong again for all of us and bring us all back together.
I have to say it one more time because of the sheer importance of this topic…SURROUND YOURSELF WITH

PEOPLE WHO LOVE YOU. I am the luckiest person on the planet to have the family I have.

You may not have kids or they may be too young to be of help to you. If they are younger than 16, I would stronger recommend not involving them. They need you to be strong and help them through. DO NOT put your kids in the middle. It can fuck with their minds. Also, DO NOT bad mouth the other person. You will want to and you will want everyone on "your side" but that is not fair to the kids or anyone else. If you love your kids protect them.

Friends

The second weekend after She left I flew to Bend, Oregon to be with my childhood friend, Carmen. For two reasons, one I needed to be in nature and away from my phone, that stupid apartment, my life. And two because Carmen is the gentlest, realest human I know. She is a hippie and a free spirit, but she also is logical about life. She gave me my space but sat quietly in the living room waiting for me. She didn't pressure me but was readily available. We spent most of the four days I was there just hiking and walking. Bend is a beautiful little mountain town with a giant river running through it. We would walk in silence for miles and if I wanted to talk, she would listen and give me her perspective. It was a very healing four days.

At home I was getting basic supportive texts from people but a couple people stood out to me. My friend Ben text me the best text I had received from anyone:

"I know you are probably sitting in hell right now, but people need you. You influence so many. Be strong for that you hold dear"

The best thing anyone said to me in those days.

He was also just there for me. In a different way than my other friends. He took me out one night, would text me and check on me and would just listen. He never gave me advice or really knew what to say, but he was there and that was all I needed.

I know I included my daughters in the "family" section but my 16-year-old daughter Triniti, who happens to be the last kid at home, had gone through a horrible break up a few months prior. She had dated Him for 3 years. He was her first everything and their relationship ended almost as abruptly as ours. She was my friend during this time. She knew what I was feeling and she would just hug me. She didn't have any words of wisdom, she just understood the hurt. I asked her to write something for this book to support what I was writing about process and her response was:

> Write that paper for me

> Here is your prompt question - What happened between you an Ash? How did you feel the first few days? The first few weeks? What helped the most and what it worse?

Mom I ain't crazy but writing that will make me

> LOL ha okay nevermind

> Someday before I get this published

I'd rather stab myself in the throat than write that

> hahaha maybe I will just screen shot this.
>
> Read 12:48 PM

It was a gift that Triniti and I had this experience together because it developed a bond between us that is unique. One unexpected friend surfaced during this time. My oldest daughter's boyfriend Davis would reach out to me almost daily and check in on me. Since he is the nicest human I have ever met and just a level headed, classy guy, everything he said gave me so much reassurance. When the kids would say I hadn't done anything wrong and that She was being a jerk to all of us, I would brush it off as emotions talking because they loved me so they couldn't be objective.

There was a time where She had said the kids were "Your kids" not Hers and that the kids never fully loved or respected her. It broke my heart and fucked with my head. I honestly couldn't remember what was truth or reality because she was saying things I had never heard before and was creating a reality we had never known. Davis was an outside perspective and told me that when he met Tay she would light up when she talked about Her and that she never said "Step-mom" she would just call Her "Mom." He explained to me that from an outside perspective we had an amazing family and an amazing relationship. He saw how much our family loved each other and he said it was beautiful, and if she couldn't see it that it was Her loss. He was a voice of reason and a lighthouse through the storm.

At work I had two confidants and angels. I only missed one day of work the first week but I left a couple hours early almost every day and while I was on the sales floor I would smile and nod and talk to people but I never heard a word they said. Since I was the head of the office it was my job to be on stage at all times, it was my job to be strong and lead by example. When I had my moments of weakness I would grab a conference room or go to the bathroom and I would just break down crying, then I would clean my face up and walk out with a smile. It was utterly exhausting. The two people who supported me at work were my training manager Carrie and my Senior Sales Director Joanna. Joanna and I had worked together at two companies and she was not only my colleague but she was also my friend. When I told her she instantly broke down in tears and kept repeating "oh my god Shianne no, oh my god" It was the most genuine visceral response I had gotten out of anyone. She held me and told me she had my back and would do anything I needed in the coming days. I felt safe, secure and loved. She was continuously there for me at work and cheered me on as I gained my strength. For the next 5 months to forever really... Joanna was my humor, my friend, my sounding board, my sister. I honestly have no idea where I would be without her. You need a Joanna ate work. Someone you can trust, who supports you unconditionally.

The second one was Carrie, we had also worked together at another company and we shared one big thing in common. We were both married to our best friend and dream person. We used to always discuss our relationships with such pride and commonality. When I told her what happened she instantly started crying, just like Joanna but this one surprised me. Although I would consider her a friend, Carrie and I weren't as close as I am with Joanna. Until now. She would come to be one of the most supportive, loving, kind people I would ever have the pleasure of knowing. In the coming days she would just ask me "How are you?" and it would help beyond measure. It's amazing how powerful and healing those three words are.

Friends and family will help you through this. We are pack animals and need the support of our pack to feel like we will survive. If they love you, they will be there. Don't be afraid to lean on them, you need them and someday they may need you. You may want to isolate yourself but that is NOT the quickest path to your badass self. Surround yourself with love and laughter!

Professionals

Before this happened I had zero desire to ever see a counselor. The second it happened I did a 180 and said "HELP ME." I saw three counselors. Yes, three. One via Skype who lived in Berkeley, California. I am a hippie at heart and I really wanted to speak to someone who believed in meditation, natural healing and would not try to prescribe me drugs. Maren was super kind, attentive and really just had a great aura about her. She was perfect for the first/worst days because she would just listen and affirm how I was feeling. I was convinced I was a horrible person and it was because I turned into a complete psycho in that fight that I lost everything. She told me a couple things that really helped, one was:

In every relationship 50% of the responsibility rests on both people. Even complacency is an action and a choice.

That day when it all happened She was cold, removed and just different. Which caused me to turn into a psychopath who kept pushing her to get her to react the way my wife would have reacted. The less she responded, the crazier I got. This reaction was eating at me because I thought it was all my fault, and She used it against me and kept telling me it was my fault. Maren's words soothed me. Personalization is a killer and a progress destroyer. If you think it is all your fault, you are wrong. Unless you randomly walked into the living room and took a bat to your partner….it is not all your fault. There is always responsibility on both sides. Which means it's not all their fault either, even if it makes you feel better in the short term to tell yourself differently, it's not all their fault.

Personalization is a killer and a progress destroyer.
If you think it is all your fault, you are wrong.

My second counselor was an older woman, whom I saw in person. She was knowledgeable and had a long career in therapy work, and COULD prescribe drugs. She used a lot of clichés and was fascinated with Her. I wanted to talk about me but she would keep bringing it back to Her. It was like she was thinking "You are strong, you'll be okay. But THIS bitch is fascinating"
She also said something that made me very uncomfortable, and the second it happened I knew it must be something I

needed to hear because it made me uncomfortable. She told me that I was more like a parent figure to Her. That I had treated her the way I treated my kids, taken care of Her and loved her deeply but it was time for Her to go learn to be on her own and find herself. This was painful because I knew it was probably true. When I met Her she was young and inexperienced and I had three kids. We were 13 years apart in age and I had already gone through so many things. I was petrified when I fell in love with her because deep down I knew she would leave me some day to go live life. Three kids for a 21 year-old is too much responsibility. There was truth in what the counselor had said and it stung. The things you resist the most are probably the things you need to dig into. Even if they are painful and you don't want to, rip the damn band-aid off.

The third counselor, was a younger therapist who was also in person. She made me step back and take a different perspective. She also made me realize that there were things within me I hadn't addressed in years. That I had lost myself and I knew I was lost and yet I had to be so strong for everyone for so long that I couldn't worry about finding me. It was eating away at me inside and since I didn't even know that it was happening I was just disintegrating as an individual. I had dealt with a bout of depression when living in San Francisco and she helped me realize that I had hung onto the depression to have a release from all of the pressure of being perfect all the time.

All three counselors served a different purpose and helped me in different ways. I am not saying you need three counselors, that may be a bit much. But go to at least one. They deal with what you are going through on a daily basis and they know how to listen and help you sort your thoughts. Sometimes it helps just talking. They aren't always right and sometimes they just grab onto some psycho analyst bullshit because they think they know where you are going in the conversation. Counselor 2 was that person. However, therapists are there for a reason and I honestly believe everyone can benefit from the experience. Try it.

Your care team is crucial, do not try to be a super hero and do this on your own. You will only end up crashing and burning later or unexpectedly in a board meeting. Humans are pack animals and they need the support of their pack when they are injured or hurt. If you have vast array of people to lean on, you won't burn out any particular individual.

Anonymous - 25 year old female

It's been three years since my dad died and then recently my boyfriend of a year broke up with me. We were long distance for the entire time, we became official right away and super serious. He told me he loved me right away and I went out there a couple weeks ago and when I got home he texted me and told me he didn't love me anymore.

My dad died three years ago and that was the biggest turning point in my life and I haven't quite dealt with it yet.

I have been very reclusive and I stay by myself. I go home and watch tv and stay by myself. I don't eat very much and I am just not happy. Both situations impacted me and it has been just one thing after another.

My darker days are me staying alone in my room, drinking and not wanting to be productive.

On my brighter days it is when I go to work, or am around people. I don't want to do it but when I do I feel a lot better. Being at work, talking to people and being around my nephew gives me a brighter day.

I really want to get married, have kids and start my life because I feel behind. I feel like I need to get back on track.

We still text and talk on the phone sometimes. But it's mostly him saying he can't do this right now and he doesn't love me anymore and it's me trying to persuade him to think about it. I think for the most part it ended because we were long distance and he wasn't giving me the attention I needed. I am still in the process of figuring out how to get over it.

I called him two nights ago, after not talking for a week, and he was really friendly and he is really nice to me. We were catching up and laughing. But then when he tells me he doesn't love me it makes it ten times worse.

When I call I am still trying to convince him to give it a try, but at least point I don't think there is any convincing.

My biggest support system is my roommate and her boyfriend. Then my mom, brother and sister.

Chapter 3

Paradigm Shifts aka "The Stages of Grief"

The night I lost you, Someone pointed me towards
The Five Stages of Grief
Go that way, they said
Its' easy, like learning to climb
stairs after an amputation
And so I climbed.
Denial was first.
I sat down for breakfast
Carefully setting the table for two
I passed you the toast-
you sat there. I passed
you the paper – you hid behind it.
Anger seemed more familiar.
I burned the toast, snatched
the paper and read the headlines myself.
But they mentioned your departure,
And so I moved on to
Bargaining. What could I exchange
for you? The silence
after storms? My typing fingers?
Before I could decide, *Depression*
Came puffing up, a poor relation
It's suitcase tied together
with string. In the suitcase
were bandages for the eyes
and bottles of sleep. I slid
all the way back down the stairs
feeling nothing. *~Linda Pastan*

Chapter 3: Paradigm Shifts aka "The Stages of Grief"

When you Google "Stages of grief" you get something like this:

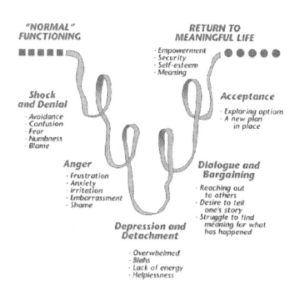

Which makes it seem like if you can get through one stage you are closer to "empowerment" a "meaningful life." I read this and I thought to myself. "Okay, I can do this. I am in denial now but there's only a few stages and I can make it through.

Little did I know.

Stages my ass. Stages dictate *a step in a process*. Unless those steps are some weird fucked up MC Escher stairs, it is definitely not a fucking stage.

The emotions are accurate but they aren't stages. They are paradigm shifts that change like the staircases in Hogwarts. You have no idea when they will change and they will most often catch you off guard and shake your footing. You will feel them randomly and they will come and go at their own will, leaving you confused and frustrated. They shift daily, hourly and sometimes minute by minute and there is no telling which one is next or if you have left one for good.

Let's go through the SHIFTS first, in no particular order.

1. Shock & Denial

If I had a dollar for every time I said "this isn't real" or "this can't be real" or "She'll come back, she has to" and SO many other denial statements, I would buy myself an Eat Pray Love trip, with maybe just the Eat part. Denial is a son of a bitch. It keeps us in a place where we are vulnerable, desperate and stagnant in our growth. The best thing you can do right now is to acknowledge:

THIS IS REAL, IT IS HAPPENING.
I CAN'T CHANGE IT BUT I CAN CHANGE HOW I REACT TO
IT.

This acknowledgement will help your mind go where it needs to in order for you to heal yourself and grow faster.
The shock part is what makes you not want to eat, makes you sick to your stomach and causes you to stare at the ceiling for hours trying to catch a single thought long enough to understand what the fuck just happened. During this shift you

will not be yourself, you will do stupid stuff, you will be very reactive or even very cold. This is a physiological response to the mental shock.

SYMPTOMS:

You will feel scared

You can't think straight

You experience physical symptoms – racing heart, upset stomach, loss of appetite, increased appetite

You feel strangely exhausted

You are "all over the place"- emotions and thoughts bouncing everywhere

You feel like and are acting like someone else

Your "upset" is so much bigger than makes logical sense.

2. Anger

The problem with this shift is it feels good. You may feel like yourself again or empowered. I had spent days in sorrow and then one day I was driving and something rushed over me where I was like *"What the fuck! I don't deserve this bullshit. I am going to be better and stronger and she will never find anyone like me"* I started saying it out loud and cheering myself on. *"Ya FUCK HER"* Oh man it felt good. I was alive again in that moment and felt strong. Ya fuck Her, I got this. I don't need Her. It felt great. It was a rush.

Until later that day when I went in for a massage and as I was laying on the table and getting all of the toxins and tension rubbed out of my body all I could think of was her soft lips, her smile, her warmth, her laughter….and down I came… sliding right back into hell. Be careful of extremes, they are tricky and they don't get you anywhere. This too is like a drug; it gives you a temporary relief that feels very real when it hits but the coming down part is a bitch.

I can say at one point during this short lived anger stint I went outside and chopped wood and I was swinging that axe like a crazy person and hitting any wood within a 5 feet radius. I chopped the shit out of everything until I was exhausted… while yelling *"FUCK THAT FUCKING BITCH"* I am not going to lie…it felt great. Probably not a bad outlet to go chop wood, be careful swinging an axe though, I had a few close calls due to my erratic technique. If you are going to chop the shit out of some wood or any other anger outlet. DO IT, put your all into it. Exhaust yourself. Then find a quiet place and let go of that anger because it does not serve YOU. It may feel good but it's merely a suppressant.

3. Depression & Detachment

My least favorite shift. Not that any of them are fun, except maybe anger, but this one is the hardest. It also hits you at the most random times. At night when you go to sleep and look at their side of the bed. When you are driving and see somewhere you went together. In the shower staring at the wall in front of me and missing when she stood there and we showered together. Looking at my own hand and remembering hers in it.

One morning I was hiking and spotted a tree she once dangled off of and it knocked the wind out of me. The "triggers" that you can't eliminate sneak up on you and rip your feet out from under you and drag you back down to hell. Simple things like pumping the gas. I was looking at the side mirror where she used to stare at me with love in her eyes. As I filled the tank I would catch her smiling and we would fall in love again. I guess objects in mirror really aren't closer than they appear after all.

Let the sadness wash over you. Let the thoughts come through, acknowledge them and let them pass freely. Don't hang onto them. Just acknowledge them and let them pass. It will be hard at first but you'll get better and better at it. Replace these thoughts with thoughts of gratitude. If you need it now, skip ahead to the chapter on Gratitude, and then come back here.

The key to overcoming the depression shift is twofold.

First – You need to realize that this will not feel this way forever. In these moments we feel like it will never end. We think there is no way we will ever smile again, ever laugh again or ever breathe again. Trust me I was 100% convinced and no one, especially not some stupid book, could convince me differently. However, it is true. This too shall pass. You will smile again, you will laugh again, you will love again. I know you don't want to hear that. I get defensive when people say that to me. "Shianne, someday you will find someone who is perfect for you."

It literally takes everything in me not to rip their faces off while screaming "SHE WAS PERFECT."

But you will, and you can't yell at me or rip my face off for saying it because I am not in the room. I get to tell you the cold hard truth and you have to read it. Well, I guess you don't. You could be like the kid in the never ending story who keeps throwing the book across the room because he doesn't like what he is reading. But we both know, you'll run over and pick it up again.

During the depression shift – you need friends the most. This is where suicidal thoughts come in and loss of worth thoughts. You need someone to remind you of your worth and the value of life.

If you are in this shift now, call your care team and got to my chapter on "Finding the will to live".

You are worth it. Life is worth it. A new adventure is waiting.

It may be winter but spring is just around the corner.

4. Dialogue & Bargaining

This shift never really ended for me during my process. I went through all the paradigm shifts while staying firmly planted in this one. I almost attached all of the texts from that month onto this book so you could see the shifts in real time. However, once I placed them into a word doc it was 132 pages. ONE HUNDRED AND THIRTY TWO PAGES of "Dialogue and bargaining."

I felt like Dr. Suess:

 "Would you love me on a hill? Would you love me if I took pills? Would you love me through this pain" would you love me in the rain?"

The answer is no. They don't love you. Or they would be with you. There is no bargaining, no negotiating. You have to acknowledge it and LET THEM GO. It's easier said than done but even if you have to do it every minute until it becomes hours, then every hour until it becomes days and then every day until those single days grow into 2 days, a week and finally a month.
Do it.
I told her goodbye at least twenty times before I finally let go. I had a calendar I would mark down. At first I couldn't go an hour. Then I made it to three hours. Then I wouldn't text her

at night. Then I went a day, two, three, four. I would mess up and text her and then spend all day texting her because it was like cheating on a diet. You know how once you fuck up you go all in because it's a "wasted day." You eat one candy bar then it turns into 5,000 calories of everything from cereal to mashed potatoes. Same thing. If I text her once, I would go crazy and text her everything. All the emotions, stories, events, begging, pleading, apologizing. I would get it all out. Then I would start my "diet" again the next day and vow to beat my prior record.

You cannot bargain your way back and what you will most likely find is that if you keep up the "dialogue" portion of this, they get the chance to unleash on you and blame everything on you because you are weak and vulnerable. I was on the phone with Her and I started in on what I thought needed to be said. Then she UNLEASHED on me. Everything was my fault, I was a horrible person, I never did this or that... I was crying and begging her to stop being mean, stop yelling at me. I was crying so hard I couldn't breathe. The harder I cried and begged, the more she yelled. I hung up because I couldn't take it. She called back, I answered because I thought she would apologize for causing me so much pain.

NOPE. She kept fucking yelling. I literally cried so hard I projectile vomited all over the bathroom because I had to run in so fast and didn't make it. I cleaned up, cleaned myself up…then filled with that fucking horrible thing called HOPE I called her back. She still yelled. I had done nothing wrong and honestly if anyone should have been yelling it should have been me. But love is funny that way, when one person is weak…the other is a piece of shit.

No more bargaining and NO more dialogue. Let it go, save yourself the time and hurt. Your diet starts now. See how long you can make it and then start again and beat your record. You got this. Day 1 – GO!

And if you cheat on your diet, it's fine. Just start again. You don't have to be perfect. You just have to NEVER GIVE UP.

5. Acceptance

This one is misleading. It isn't as grand and peaceful as it sounds. You may come to the point of acceptance but still be deeply sad. Once I accepted the fact that it was over and she wasn't coming back, it didn't change the sadness I felt and the hurt. I just quit bargaining, anger etc.. Also, this shift is like a fucking magnet for the ex. As soon as you come into this shift there is a really good chance they will reach out to you. Its' like a sick sense. I know it's a "sixth sense," but it's sick to me. They can feel when you are feeling better and they will text you or call you on an upswing and knock you all the way down again.

THE WORST is the "let's be friends" bullshit. No bitch I don't want to be your friend. You ripped my heart out, stomped on it continually, left me and my kids heart broken, didn't care if I lived or died...pretty sure I have enemies nicer than you.

You CANNOT be friends with your ex. At least not now. There is too much shit involved and you have too much work to do.

They want to be your friend and they try to make you feel guilty about it because it makes it EASIER FOR THEM. Well fuck them.

They will just reopen your wounds and you'll have to start all over again.

That's why during this shift it is absolutely CRUCIAL that you DO NOT CONTACT THEM OR RESPOND. It is CRUCIAL.

Also, don't overestimate your strength. This shift gives you a false sense of strength and ability. You think you can look at that photo album, you think you can see them.

YOU CAN'T

IT IS NOT TIME AND YOU ARE NOT READY

You may think you are. You could be feeling good, strutting and optimistic about your new found freedom.

NOPE.

Acceptance is an illusion. It takes a lot of time for real acceptance to come in. Even when I was driving along, smiling and singing again…She would creep into my mind and fuck up my head and send me right back down. I sent her a final text when I feeling confident and knew it was over. I was accepting the fate of the situation with peace and clarity. I said "I love you with all my heart, goodbye" she replied "I love you too, goodnight"

WHAT THE FUCK IS THAT???

They love to keep you hanging on and you love to let them. It's like when you think that scab has healed and its itching you, so you just decide to peel it off…but then it hurts like hell, starts bleeding again…and now it's going to take another 3 days to heal again…and great now it's going to scar.

DON'T PICK THAT SCAB! ITS NOT READY!

The shifts or "stages" will bounce all over the place and can be triggered by different things. I personally stayed in the bargaining shift, but anger might be your shift, or maybe denial. Regardless of where your main paradigm is, you will need to eventually move on. You cannot be angry forever, you cannot be in denial forever and you definitely cannot beg them to come back forever. There has to come a time where you let go. By journaling you will be able to observe the shifts and understand what sets each one off and how you get through them.

The time that it takes for real letting go to happen may be over a long period of time, or it could happen in an instant. My letting go moment was very clear and very memorable. My 19 year old daughter Jasmine came over to visit and we were hanging out and talking ….not about Her….just life, how's work etc…. Then Jasmine just stopped, dropped her head and started bawling (It sneaks up on you). I held her close for two hours as she cried in my lap. I was hurt for her and desperate to help heal her…Then something miraculous happened. I knew I had to let go of Her because of how it was effecting my daughter, my family. I had to let Her go. I had to. I didn't just want to, I had to. I knew it with everything in me.

It didn't relieve the sadness or the pain but there was a peace in knowing I had to let go. Somehow once the "hope" was gone, the healing began. It was still a process but it was much better. Hope is the nail in the road to peace. You will be driving along smoothly and HOPE hits you, blows your tire and send you spiraling into the nearest tree.

Abandon hope. Let it go.

Even if you do get back together someday, you don't need hope to get there. You need strength, perseverance and perspective. But not hope. It is the devil that makes you stare at the phone, makes you give them things they don't deserve, makes you beg and keeps you weak.

It is important that you take this part very serious.

If you want more strength right now, more strength tomorrow...ABANDON HOPE.

You have to recognize the truth in the situation and the truth is:

It is OVER.

Life will go on.

This pain will not last forever.

This is NOT your fault.

You are worthy of love.

You will be happy again.

That is the truth.

Anonymous – Female - 36

I met a guy at 29 years old from Cincinnati on a sales trip from Phoenix to NY. I decided to move my entire life to be with this guy I invested time, all of my money and savings into a relationship that was not vested, we were not married. I moved away from all of my friends and family for this guy and the promise of a future. Great relationship, no arguing, no fighting, no issues with money or anything of the sort.

At the three-year period, we had bought this old historic house and although I had invested financially he had put it in his name. Right after we moved in my mom came to visit, and help us get it all fixed up and remodeled. When she leaves, she flies out at 11a. and he breaks up with me ten hours later in bed during watching a football game. It was a very casual conversation. He started with "I need to talk to you, I don't want to be with you anymore" I was floored and totally shocked.

There was no reason, nothing leading up to this to give me any indication of what was coming. So, of course like anybody that is surprised and hurt I asked "Why? What did I do? What could I do better?" He replied with "I don't have to give you a reason." I pushed and pushed and told him I needed closure. He said "This closure is for you," you can feel however you want to feel or think whatever you want to think about why it is coming to an end. I don't want to be with you and I don't have to give you a reason."

Well of course, thinking I would be able to change his mind, I stayed in a house where I was not wanted in a city where I had no one. Changing careers, giving up everything and finally realizing that I needed to pack my car and go back home. By the end of the three weeks I was no longer looking for him to say I want to be with you, I was still searching for the reason. So I come back to Phoenix and I am broken, I lose 20 lbs, I am tired, I don't know what I want to do career wise. I surrounded myself with family and friends which lead me to get back to work and teaching and just trying to put myself out there.

The one thing that always stuck with me was that I had never had closure, because this guy never gave me a reason. When I finally realized that I didn't need him or want him, it was clear to me that you don't have to give someone a reason. If you don't want to be with them, that's it. The reason is for closure on their part, not for you. I would still say it's a selfish move, but of course it's a choice. That's the only lesson I took away from that relationship. Regardless of what is going on at the end of the relationship you don't have to tell the other person why, but if your respect them you should.

Nobody can make you "feel" anyway. They can say things and it obviously has an effect but ultimately you decide how you react. If someone doesn't want to be with you or give you a reason, you have to find that closure for yourself. It is so much harder to find closure in a situation where you can't quite pinpoint what the problem was.

I started to feel good again at the three month mark. Not good, but myself. First and foremost you need people, you need to feel love and you need to feel wanted. I had to love myself and that was about the 6 month mark.

Now looking back, I know why he couldn't give me an answer. Three month prior to the breakup I had introduced him to my banker because he had started a small business and needed to open an account. They are now married. I believe from the moment I introduced them he was thinking of how to get out of the relationship with me. When we broke up I asked him if he was interested in her and he told me I was crazy. Well if we know anything, if your partner or significant other is calling you crazy, its only them deflecting the truth from what they have done. And sure enough a month later he called me about shipping my stuff and I asked him if he was seeing anyone and he admitted to dating her. Now they are married and they have a kid.

I know now what my answer is, but it took time and in the meantime it led me to a better place. It's going to lead you to a better place but you may not know your reason for quite some time.

Chapter 4

When the Tears Come

The pain is unbearable

My heart is broken, destroyed

even my skin hurts

My head is heavy

with the weight of

thoughts of you.

My soul is lost

somewhere inside me

searching..

I try to grab onto…

anything

There is nothing

left in me

anywhere

Where are you

What did I do to

deserve

so much pain.

~ by Me at week 3

Chapter 4: When the tears come

In the beginning the tears are non-stop. I live in Arizona and it was spring when it happened so it was already HOT and I was crying constantly. I had no idea how I did not die of dehydration. The tears come in all forms. It's like in Forest Gump when he describes the rain.

There's little bitty stinging tears, big fat tears, tears that seem to come up from under you.

There would be tears streaming down my cheeks and I had no idea I was crying. I was driving my scooter once and the tears always stream out of my eyes a little from the wind. However, this time they were just flowing and flowing and when I finally stopped at a light I realized I was in full blown crying fit. I would wake up from crying. I'd be dead asleep and wake up with a fully wet face and the fucking painful stomach wrenching crying. I'm pretty sure I was "sleep" crying for a good minute or so before I even woke up.

There will be times when you feel happy–ish and you'll be going about your day and then random bullshit just hits you like a brick and you lose your shit out of nowhere. I got on the phone with Her to discuss the divorce. I was feeling strong and happy, I made it through like a champ. As the conversation went on I got a false sense of security and started talking to her about other things….bad idea. All the emotions came and I turned into a bumbling, crying idiot. I spent the rest of the day and night texting her like crazy, begging for her love and finally crying myself to sleep.

You are probably crying now, just thinking about crying.

Let me make something perfectly clear. The tears are good. They are healthy. You need to let them flow, most of the time. There will be times however, that it's not the time or place. Example: standing in front of 100 people talking about the results from the month before in an All Hands meeting. Definitely not the time.

There will be times where you will allow the tears to flow, just to release the emotions. Then you find yourself in a full blown painful, wailing episode that you can't recover from. You grab onto the pillow, your stomach, your head, you'll grab anything to hang onto for dear life. Laying in a fetal position and just hurting from head to toe.

To overcome these moments and get back on your feet, here are some tricks that I used.

First, I hope you have eliminated all the "triggers" and you aren't listening to sad music or watching some stupid romantic movie. If so, that's your problem. Turn it off and go for a walk or run.

If not and it's a random crying fit at work, first get out of the situation, room etc...If you can. Go to the bathroom, let it out. Wash your face. Then look in the mirror, smile and say:

"Nope, I am done crying. It is a good day. I am strong. I am better than this. It's going to be a good day"

Then keep that smile and go right back to work. Work is GREAT. It is so distracting. Everyone told me to take time off but at work I was so distracted, I only would cry discretely a couple times a day and then I went right back to work. It was going home to an empty apartment that I dreaded.

If you are in a situation where you can't exit stage left...think of something funny as quickly as possible. Your favorite funny video, something the person is saying or imagine them naked. (Old public speaking trick). Just pivot your thoughts quickly completely away from whatever you are thinking. Sing the ABC's in your mind in Elmo's voice. Whatever it takes to distract yourself. In my opinion humor works best.

The other trick I used was counting to 5. I learned it from Mel Robbins book "The Five Second Rule." It's the world's simplest concept but it works. She talks about using it to make decisions and be bolder in life. It works great to stop the crying fits. Right in the middle of your tears, do this: Think: I don't want to sit here and suffer right now. On the count of five I am going to pick myself up, wipe the tears off, smile, be grateful and STOP CRYING. Count to 5 and then at 5 you have to FORCE YOURSELF to stop and follow those steps. Not at 5.5 seconds or 6 seconds. When you hit 5 STOP. Another trick, just like sad music makes you spiral down. Put on a happy song that makes you dance. Music is so healing and can really move us emotionally, that's why you cannot and should not listen to sad songs. Even songs that come off as happy like "Always be my baby" by Mariah Carey, great beat, horrible lyrics....

Put on something silly that makes you dance and has nothing to do with love.

Old school – "Call me Al" by Paul Simon, "Don't stop me now" by Queen, "Survive" Diana Ross

New – "Happy" Pharell Williams, "Send me on my way" Mystic Roots

I was really digging "Love myself" by Hailee Steinfield. That one got me going.

There are so many out there that are just fun, turn them on, turn them up. Laugh, dance like an idiot. Fake it til you make it!

Be careful throwing on any old Pandora station though. I had on Blink 182 which seemed like a safe choice. Then in the middle of a five mile run, Green Day's "Time of your life' came on. I won't torture you by putting the lyrics in here but let's just say it fucking sucked. I was running, my phone was in my hip bag and I couldn't instantly change it. Who am I kidding, I let it play and I sang it in my head.

Crying while running = puking. Tip from me to you.

Laughter really is the best medicine for tears. There is a really old movie called "Steel Magnolia's" that my mom loved, it has a scene where the main character, played by Sally Field, has a daughter who dies. She is at the funeral with her group of friends and it is the saddest scene ever. Sally field's character is crying and desperate over the loss of her daughter, then right in the middle of this heart wrenching scene one of the ladies grabs their friend and tells Sally Field to PUNCH HER, PUNCH HER! DO IT! And the group of women all go from tears to laughter.

Find the funny. Find your joy. Be around funny humans, people who make you laugh. Watch funny videos. They are healing to your soul.

Knock knock. Who's there? Smell mop. (finish this joke in your head)

Chapter 5

Finding the will to live – dealing with suicidal thoughts

Today
I Choose to sit quietly in the sun and watch copper winged dragonflies
I Choose to be still and listen
I Choose to be open to whatever presents itself
I Choose to be kind and refrain from judgement of others
I Choose to drink copious amounts of tea
I Choose to purge my thoughts and feelings and write write write until there is nothing left inside to come out
I Choose to smile at everyone and not care if they think "Who is this crazy smiling lady and what is she so happy about?"
I Choose to project <u>happiness</u> into the coming week
I <u>Choose</u> not to allow other's insecurities and fears infect me with self-doubt
I Choose to take time throughout the day and send heartfelt virtual hugs to those I care about
I Choose to accept this moment, right now, and savor the essence before it slips away
I Choose to step with love, creating a safe path in hopes that others will join me on my journey
I Choose to stand tall (a full five feet 2 inches), face life head on, saying "C'mon! Gimmee all you got!! Don't hold back because I can handle it!"
Then I wait and listen…Life says: "Well, ok then- here it goes! Brace yourself!"
I do, it comes…and you know what?
I am still standing.

• Elif Elkin

Chapter 5: Finding the will to live - dealing with suicidal thoughts

My cousin committed suicide a few years ago and I remember thinking how selfish it was that she did that to her kids. It's funny how you judge people if you have not walked in their shoes. I never thought depression was a real thing either, I thought people were weak and needed to man up and own their shit. Until depression hit me when I was living in SF and it was like a cloud of darkness that would just follow me around and anytime I got a glimpse of the sun it would just slowly cover it up and shroud my whole world in gloom again.

As for suicide, it briefly crossed my mind at harder times but like a fleeting thought that passes through as quickly as it arrives. It's not real and you would never do "it" but it occurs to you from time to time how nice it would be to not have to deal with life but then you move on.

During the first two weeks of my hell I hardly thought of anything else. Not in a dramatic hand to forehead fainting motion, "my life is over" kind of way. It just seemed like a very logical next step.

I told myself:

I have lived my life. I have accomplished so much. I raised amazing kids. Had the perfect relationship. I have built a successful career. Lived in epic places. Owned houses, nice cars. Had the dream life. So it's time to go. There is nothing left for me. I just don't want to live.

I rationalized it.

I am the least selfish person I know, everything I have ever done has been for everyone else, all the time. If I want this, everyone should support me. It's so selfish of everyone else to want me to live through this pain. It's not fair. I should be able to end my own life if I want to. It's my life. The kids all have their own lives and will all get marred one day and I will be all alone. She will never come back and I don't want to live without Her so why should I?

The rationalization went on and on. Luckily Liam was by my side daily and would just say "Nope." He would let me say all these things and vent and cry and he would simply say "nope." It was infuriating.

It helped me, but what completely changed my mind was when I apologized to my oldest daughter Taylor for having ever felt that way and she broke down crying and laid her head on my lap. I looked down at her pain and realized how stupid I was being. I had so much to live for. I had amazing, perfect kids who loved me very much. We have a kick ass family and so many good times. I have my beautiful kids, my mom, Liam, my friends. Also, if I did this She would win. She would break me, break my kids, break so many people. I heard a quote in some motivational video on Youtube, I have no idea who said it but it went "Suicide doesn't end pain, it transfers it." Meaning if I ended my life my pain would be over but my children and my family would take on that pain. How fucked up is that to do to people?

It was in my daughter's pain that I released the desire to end my life and I vowed I would never go there again. Never. I worked for 22 years to create an amazing life for my family and to parent these kids into outstanding humans. I had succeeded and it was my greatest accomplishment and I could have destroyed everything and everyone in the blink of an eye, and for what? Some stupid, selfish human who didn't love any of us anyway?

Some interesting things came out of going through this feeling.

First, I used to be so scared of my own mortality. I couldn't even think about life ending because it would make me so sad and scared. Especially after meeting Her. Forever wasn't enough with Her and the thought of dying one day and ending our time together just crushed my insides. Now, although I am so happy to be alive and I love my life, my family, myself; but I am not scared to die. I am okay with it. There is a sense of relief and peace that came from going through such a close call with death. It's almost like an understanding with the universe that nothing lasts forever. Not true love and not life. So enjoy every minute while it lasts.

Second, if I would have ended my life I would not have written this book and I wouldn't have the opportunity to help you right now. Isn't that crazy? YOU saved ME. You did. The fact that you are holding something I wrote from my heart during the worst experience of my life, so that I can help you through your worst experience....WOAH. Best thing that has ever happened to me. Which means…it is your turn now. Your turn to help someone else. It's going to be like this awesome heart break, badass pay it forward if you let it.

Just because it is the end of ONE story for you, doesn't mean the next story won't be even better.

In this moment I want you to do something:

Write three things you love about yourself

1.

2.

3.

Name 3 people who you deeply love (NOT the ex)

1.

2.

3.

Now write three things you love about your life

1.

2.

3.

Now write three things on your bucket list that you always wanted to do

1.

2.

3.

Now read all of those things out loud.

In 5 quick minutes you came up with 12 reasons to live. You have reasons to live. Even if in your stubborn pain right now you only wrote one single thing down...it is still a reason. I know that if you are stubborn like me, you may have written stupid things like "I am happiest with them" That's definitely some shit I would do. Now go back and actually THINK of a time when you were happy BEFORE THEM.
You will use these positive thoughts to help yourself see there is so much to live for.
This pain is temporary. Quitting is forever. You are NOT a quitter. You are better than that.

Don't be afraid to reach out for help if you can't get these thoughts under control. I told my counselors what I was feeling, I told Liam. I told my journal. Be careful telling people that it could hurt irreparably. I should have never told my mom or my kids. Even though my kids are all adults, it was unfair and a horribly heavy weight for them to bear. I acknowledged my path of thinking to them afterward and explained they were real emotions but it was ignorant of me to have ever gone there. I told them there is so much good in this life and while I lost sight of it for a second, their love and being with them reminded me. I also promised I would never allow myself to go down that dark path of thinking again. There are also suicide hotlines. I never used one but I imagine it is a bit like free counseling. Whatever resources are out there, feel free to use them.

There were times where I thought if I killed myself She would have to go through what I am going through. I wondered if She would even care. I also told Her consistently what I was thinking to see if she would react.

One night for the FIRST time I was NOT actually thinking of killing myself and I just wanted to sleep for once, so I took 3 sleeping pills and drank 3 shots of vodka. I am a fairly little person and I never drink so I thought that would definitely do it. I woke up 2 hours later!!! So, I took 3 more sleeping pills, and never went back to sleep. I text her this time and told her, just to get a reaction. All I got was "Stop" and "Don't do that." That was it, nothing until a day later, she never even checked on me. The love of my life didn't even care if I lived or died, now that was a hard "pill" to swallow.

The funny thing is, the times I told her stuff like that were the times I wasn't actually going to do it. It was the times where I sat alone, not talking to anyone and staring at the wall....those times I would literally walk through the best way. I sat in the bathtub, holding a razor blade and staring at my wrists. Quietly, not telling anyone. Then I imagined my 16-year-old daughter, Triniti, who is the last one at home, coming in and finding me. I couldn't do that to her. I turned the water off, cried until the water went cold and then lifted myself out of that tub. My counselor had said that children of parents who commit suicide are exponentially more likely to kill themselves. Her words rang in my head.

Also, if you are doing this to see if They care, it's pathetic. Trust me. I was pathetic. They won't give you the reaction you want and if they do...once they know you are okay they are still gone. These are not the renaissance times, it's not a romantic gesture. You threatening to end your life makes you look weak and no one wants to be with someone who is weak. It also won't hurt them. You want to hurt them? Be HAPPY without them. There is your revenge.

The key to getting through these times is to find something that is stronger than the desire to die. Find a "will" anchor. Something to imagine. Suicide is easy for the individual, but it is the people who are left behind who are effected.

Plus, your future badass self would slap those pills out of your hand and tell you to get the fuck up and knock your shit off. My "Will" anchor is my children. Imagining what it would do to them.

Let go of these thoughts and when they come in use your "Will" anchor that you found to keep you grounded in reality. In life, if things are always easy we never really learn or grow. As horrible as this time is for you right now, you are going through a cathartic experience. Your rawest emotions are out and your soul is bare. When you make it through this, you will be stronger and a more experienced human. It's like running...its sucks and it can hurt and you want to quit...but if you don't and you make it through the miles...you feel amazing. You will be healthier, stronger and you feel accomplished. This is WAY harder than running, so imagine the reward in store for you.

In the end the best revenge on anyone is to go have a better life than what you had with them. In the badass chapters you will learn how to find your best self within and create a fulfilled enriched life.

Life sucks right now but it will not suck forever. I promise.

Chapter 6

Stop Blaming Yourself

When there is no enemy from within

The enemy outside cannot hurt you. ~ African proverb

Chapter 6: Stop blaming yourself

Jessica is the best friend of my oldest daughter and one of the kindest sweetest people you could ever meet. She had been dating a guy for over a year who she adored and who treated her like shit. My daughter hated the guy from the minute she met him, but Jessica held on to the belief that he was a good guy. Even on Jessica's 21st birthday in Vegas this guy made the whole trip all about him and his needs, while Jess quietly sat by.

A month later she was devastated when she found out that for their entire relationship he had a girlfriend that he had been with for 3 years. This happened to her right before my wife left me. Since Jessica is my target demographic for this book, I asked her to read it and give my any feedback she might have. This is the text she sent me after reading my earliest draft:

Hey, I just finished reading. I don't know if you had specific questions for whoever reads it but I made a note to tell that I would really love to read more about the blaming yourself part. I am always first to blame myself. It's ALWAYS my fault in my head.

Anyone from the outside would 100% know that Jess was not to blame in the demise of her relationship with that asshole. She is sweet, kind, selfless and accommodating. He was a selfish piece of shit who was dating two girls simultaneously. And yet, Jess swore it was her fault.

I really fucked up that day when we argued. I told Her to leave, I bought her plane ticket. I kept pushing her to respond. I never said anything mean in any way but I just kept pushing her out. The next day I knew I fucked up and begged her for the next 7 weeks to love and forgive me. I ran that day over in my head a million times. I had been horrible; I knew I was to blame. I should have never told her to leave. I should have begged her to stay and supported her. I immediately apologized and took the blame... she spent the next 7 weeks blaming me too.

In the heat of emotion taking the blame was natural, but now looking back after countless books, counselors and friends I know that even though I pushed her that ONE day I had been amazing to her for 8 years before that. Anyone in my shoes, when watching the love of your life mentally walk away would panic and do things they would probably regret. She would have left regardless of how I acted that day. She had already left mentally the weekend before and now since I was freely taking the blame she was freely able to give it to me so it would be easier for Her.

It's funny because now that I am rational I know that if the tables were reversed and I was the cold one who was leaving and if I was numb to her emotions, she would have reacted way worse than I did because she has a temper. She was always quick to get mad in the past and took things really personally. Until this day I had never gotten mad at her or raised my voice.

We take the blame because it's controllable. I can't control what she did, how she felt or how she acted. I can however, control me. So therefore in order to have some sense of control in a chaotic situation I took the blame. Jess couldn't control her ex, she couldn't control his lies, his deceit, his selfishness…but in her mind she could control what she did. So, maybe if she was better or more loveable …something… anything… he would have saw value in her and never treated her so poorly.

We also do something called *personalization*, which is when we believe that when others do or say something it is a direct association to what we have done or said. My counselor gave me the best example.

You know when the teacher says "I just had my pencil lying here on the desk and it is gone"

All the hands go up not to say where it went but to say "I didn't take it!"

We automatically associate ourselves with statements and actions, and quickly try to defend ourselves.

Now here is the tricky part...it is not all their fault either.

There are two common stances that people take.

1. It's all MY fault.

2. It's all THEIR fault.

Newsflash: Neither are true.

One person may be more responsible for sure. In Jess's case, the guy was an asshole and she deserved better. Everyone knows that. But, her responsibility is to be able to recognize that and not let someone treat her that way.

It is up to us to know our worth and not allow people to treat us less than our worth.

In my case I took ALL the blame at first, then I realized She walked out on 8 years of an amazing relationship. She left our kids, didn't even say goodbye and hurt so many people. It didn't matter what I did that day, she never even tried once to fight for us or try to fix it. She used it as an escape. After 8 years she didn't even care if I lived or died. She never once tried.

Nothing I did in that one fight created that within her.

I want to believe there is something I could do differently, but there isn't. She left for something in her and it has nothing to do with me.

They left you for something that is happening within them and that is their responsibility, not yours.

bad·ass

'bad‚ass

noun

1.   a tough, uncompromising, or intimidating person.

The devil whispered in my ear,

"You're not strong enough to withstand the storm."

Today I whispered in the devil's ear

"I am the storm."

Ready for Badass?

During my "Broken" days I just wanted to know when I would stop hurting, when I would breathe again, when I would able to go a whole day without crying. Then, I started to talking to people about their stories and there were people who told me it took, months or years to get over their ex. That shook me, months of this bullshit? Years? Are you fucking kidding me? I remember saying out loud…"I will fucking shoot myself if I still feel like this in a year from now." I made a decision in that moment that I would give myself two months to mourn, cry, do whatever I needed to heal…then I am moving the fuck on. (I backslide at the two-month mark and set my goal on 5 months. I hit that goal!)

One day just before the two month mark She called me and although it typically would send me spiraling back into sadness and desperation when we talked, this time was different. We talked about casual things like plans for the weekend and updates on each other's lives. She told me she had put together a bookshelf from Walmart and was so proud of herself, other than that she hadn't really done anything with herself in the two months she had been gone. It was also a

Saturday night and she was home cooking...correction... burning a turkey burger. She left me to go "LIVE" and she was home on a Saturday night by herself.

When I hung up something miraculous happened...I laughed. I realized I deserved better than someone who would leave me and our children for the accomplishment of putting together a Walmart bookshelf and the joy of a burnt turkey burger. I deserved better than someone who would hurt me so deeply, hurt my kids so deeply and never even bat an eyelash. It didn't matter what we had in the past, that was gone and was never coming back. I had to realize my present and it was time to give my love to someone else....me. To be clear, I had several "moments" of letting go, but after each one I became stronger.

These chapters are for later stages in your journey. The first couple days you will probably be too raw, too lost in emotion to fully digest or appreciate these chapters. Maybe not though, who am I to tell you? You could already be badass and just need a boost. If so, go for it.

You could feel ready for the badass portion and you'll jump right in. If you backslide and need a tears reminder, or just a back to basics survival reminder…go back to the Broken chapters and find what you need.

The Badass portion isn't about riding a Harley, with tattoos and kicking ass kind of "badass," unless that is your true self, then fuck ya go for it. It is about using this cathartic experience to reach down within and find the truest version of yourself. It is about taking this as an opportunity to catapult yourself into drastic change that would have either never come or would have taken a long period of time.

When you are laid bare and your defenses are down, you are primed to look inside and see what you need to change. In every relationship we lose a piece of ourselves because we mold and mesh our lives into the other person. It's not necessarily a bad thing. However, that little lost piece is just waiting to be found. It is time to love yourself.

I only wanted Her all the time. I didn't care to have friends or go anywhere she wasn't. I didn't write as much, didn't run as much. I would be totally happy wrapped in her arms day after day in our bed. Then I was left without my favorite past time, without my soul, without a purpose. I was left alone and I was alone with a stranger. I didn't even recognize myself anymore.

I had always been a strong woman that lead people, helped others, and had people look up to me. I wasn't afraid of anything and I knew my worth and capability…then suddenly I was a pathetic crying mess with no direction in life. During this time I realized that things I was naturally being drawn to in the first few days, were the things that I use to love in life. I was thrown into self-discovery, and I discovered I actually missed me. I was drawn to nature, writing, reading. I lost weight, okay not eating helped, but I was also running every day. I was listening to music, meditating and thinking. I had never taken time for myself before and now time alone was all I had. It was uncomfortable at first but then I remembered something powerful… I LOVE ME.

As you become your badass self you will realize your badass self is most likely the version of yourself you knew existed years ago or that you know exists now but you have been too busy to tap into it. There is greatness within you and in the following chapters we will be pulling it out of you, shining it up and making yourself badass again.

And remember…sometimes badass is not letting anyone break you. Sometimes it is simply waking up every day, continuing on your path and refusing to give up.

Chapter 1

Embracing The Experience – there is beauty within the pain

When you come out of the storm, you won't be the same person that walked in. That's what the storm is all about" –

Haruki Murakami

Chapter 1: Embracing The Experience – there is beauty within the pain

The title of this chapter alone is a good example of why you need to be further on through the darkest days before reading these chapters. If I would have read this in days 1-3 I would have burned this book.

 "Beauty within the pain" are you fucking kidding me? I am a disaster and there's nothing beautiful about days of tears puffy face, snot, no sleep. There is definitely nothing beautiful about the end of a perfect love story with a tragic twisted fucked up ending. There isn't anything beautiful about kids who are hurt and a family that is broken.

And yet…. there is. At about day ten I wrote in my journal that:

This experience is absolutely horrible, I have never felt so much pain and endured so much deep deep sorrow in my entire life. My worst fears have been realized and I am lost and broken. And yet…it is a stunningly beautiful experience. I cannot believe a human can go through this and survive. I am finding out so much about myself, about who my real friends are and what I genuinely want deep in my soul

Of course I went right back into writing about Her and emotions etc. but even in the depths of despair I knew that something magical could happen, if I let it. It's weird. You know how when you fall in love for the first time it opens your eyes to the whole world and you just GET things that you didn't fully understand before? Or when you have kids....there are so many ah ha moments. There are just things in life that you have to experience first-hand and you cannot create. It has to be organic.

There is a scene in the movie Good Will Hunting where Robin Williams character who is a therapist tells the young genius Will Hunting that although he may be smart, he will never fully understand life until he experiences it, pain and all. The scene is intense and it shuts the cocky kid up. Here is the speech:

I ask you about war, and you'd probably throw Shakespeare at me right? "Once more into the breach, dear friends" But you've never been near one. You've never held your friends head in your lap and watched him gasp his last breath, looking to you for help. And if I asked you about love you'd probably quote me a sonnet. But you've never looked at a woman and been totally vulnerable. Known someone who could level you with her eyes, feeling like God put an angel on earth just for you...who could rescue you from the depths of hell. And you wouldn't know what it's like to be her angel and to have that love for her to be there forever. Through anything. Through cancer. You wouldn't know about sleeping sitting up in a hospital room for two months holding her hand because the doctors could see in your eyes that the term, "visiting hours" doesn't apply to you. You don't know about real loss, because that only occurs when you love something more than yourself.

I thought I knew heartbreak before Her. I had been in relationships and been hurt but I had never experienced the pain that She put me through. I have never known what all the sonnets of loss have truly been about, the tears of millions of people before me. The pain of hundreds of generations. I never knew what it was to love someone so much you die inside. I thought I did. I genuinely thought I had experienced hut. But it's like getting a cut on your finger and saying you know what getting your arm chopped off would be like. The attorney that I spoke with likened the experience to being like a death, but one that is on purpose. That is best description I have heard to explain the way it felt.

You probably had no clue what love means, what hurt means...until now and there is something exquisitely beautiful about that.

As hard as it is right now for you to understand, something beautiful is happening to you. Like a caterpillar in a cocoon. The cocoon is ugly and brown and the caterpillar is shrouded in darkness and isolation. Yet, it triumphs, pushes through and emerges more beautiful than ever and then something magical happens...IT CAN FLY. It can only fly if it can fight its way out of the cocoon though. If you try to help it and you open the cocoon for it because it looks like its struggling so much...the wings won't be strong enough to fly without the fight.

Winter is cold and everything dies, the birds stop chirping, the ground freezes and everything turns brown. But winter leads to spring and flowers bloom, the grass looks greener than ever and everything is new again. Spring wouldn't be as beautiful if it were eternal. It's so beautiful because we made it through the dark and cold.

I was watching a documentary about San Francisco and the AIDS epidemic of the twentieth century. One of the AIDs victims said that life became more beautiful to him as his mortality became more evident. He realized that life was so beautiful and precious because he was mortal. It was like someone lifted a fog and from then on he cherished every moment. On his death bed he said that he wouldn't take the experience back because his last years were his best years.

You could spend years writing and exploring and setting goals but it won't create the change that these moments will. This is real and raw and you my friend are more pliable than ever.

Grab your journal. It's time for a writing exercise. You are going to do a chain of thought exercise. You are going to write for 20 minutes. Set a timer. No stopping. Don't worry about punctuation, run on sentences. Just flow.
This writing is about you. NOT THEM.

If you find yourself writing about them…pivot and bring it back to you.

Okay here is the prompt:

Who am I?

What do I love (not them)?

If I could do anything with my time what would it be?

When am I the happiest? (DO NOT WRITE "WITH THEM")

Okay set a timer – 20 minutes – GO.

Now look back at what you wrote and read it aloud. Circle the things that make you the most excited or happy. Those are the things you will focus on in the coming days as you realize your badass self and life.

Write the top 3 here:

1.

2.

3.

Did you discover anything about yourself that you didn't know? Maybe not. But I bet that you discovered that you have forgotten to take care of you. There is a great book by Sark titled "Succulent Wild Woman" and she gives great examples of how to love and take care of yourself. She says to take yourself on dates, pamper yourself and romance yourself. I read it after my first divorce from a horrible relationship where I was completely subservient to the man I was married to. She taught me to love me. Then I read it again after losing the love of my life. Sark reminded me that I still have me to love and care for. She tells you to take yourself on dates and be good to yourself. Through it all I will always stick by my side. I have learned to be a great friend to myself. Treat yourself the way you would treat a best friend.

That is where the true beauty lies. Loving yourself.

The time where I was broken and hurting, I was also so deeply alive and open to change and the energies of life. I am happy now, no more tears, no more pain. I love life and all of it's possibilities…and somehow there is a tiny piece of me that misses my spirit during the broken times. I am not saying I ever want to go through that again, hell no. But it was genuinely a beautiful time and I was so raw and open to the world that it was like going through a crash course in self-discovery. I learned so much about myself, I found ways to love myself, I figured out what I wanted and what I didn't in life. It was a gift, that I will always look back on with appreciation for the beauty within the pain. Someday, if you approach this right. You will too.

Your EX may have told you that you are _____(Something negative). Maybe right now you are sitting here thinking "something negative" about yourself that they told you that you were, or maybe it is what you tell yourself you are.
Let's take that out and examine it for truth

What is bad about you?

Did they say that or you?

Is it true? How?

The truth is this only is true if you believe it, if you continue to allow it to have power over you.
She left me and then she spent the next few months trying to tear me down because it made her feel better. It helped the guilt she felt by placing blame on me and telling me I was selfish, judgmental and that I held her back in life. It ate away at my brain because I always loved her so much and always

wanted what she wanted. I had to take a step back and realize her words only had power over me if I LET THEM. I did a self-evaluation and realized that out of everyone I knew – 99 of them would say I am the most selfless person they know, but because the one person I loved so deeply said I was selfish I wanted to believe it. I wanted to believe it because it felt better having something in my control that I could change. The truth was She was projecting. She had made a choice that hurt someone she promised to love forever and even worse….a choice that not only hurt kids but impacted the way they view love and commitment forever. BUT humans don't want to believe that in themselves so they project onto others.

Now ask yourself, what have they said about you?

Examine it for truth. Maybe it is true. Then how will you change it? And do you want to change it? Should you?

She also hated how driven I was, she hated that I wanted to conquer the world and I always had goals and never stopped pushing forward. Which is fine, that might be too much for some people. But after examining it I discovered that I don't want to change that. That drive within me is what gave me strength to endure an abusive relationship, to raise three amazing children on my own, to go to college when no one in my family had, to be bold enough to move out of our comfort zone and work hard to provide my family a life I didn't have. My drive helped me moved up in my career and take so many people with me. My drive gave my family experiences and adventures that most people haven't experienced. My drive helped me through this hell, my drive helped me write this book.

I don't want to change that within myself and if She didn't like it that is fine. It is who I am and I won't apologize for it anymore and I won't tear myself down so other people can feel better about themselves.

DO NOT TEAR YOURSELF DOWN FOR ANYONE.

Answer these:

What is my strength?

What is within me that someone may have perceived as negative but actually makes me who I am?

What can I do daily to further develop my strengths?

There is beauty within the pain and there is beauty and strength within you. Find it and use it.

Chapter 2

Fake it til you make it

You must be the person you have never had the courage to be. Gradually, you will discover that you are that person, but until you can see this clearly, you must pretend and invent. –

Paulo Coelho

Chapter 2: Fake it til you make it

When I was interviewing people for the book, I spoke to a divorce attorney who had been in business for over 16 years in Scottsdale. She had seen so many broken hearts come into her office and watched all the stages happen in real time with countless individuals. I asked her about the people that were the most broken in the beginning but made the fastest recovery and what had they done differently. Her response was:

"I have had a couple people recover quickly and it was the "Fake it, until you feel it" kind of thing. They would pretend that they were fine and you knew that they weren't but eventually they were fine. Some that I have actually become very good friends with. People who just tell themselves they are good until they actually are sure of it."

In the first weeks of my hell I would have people who kept telling me that they couldn't believe how strong I was being or how fast I recovered. Most of the time in the early days I was just really good at faking it. I would smile and say "Ya, you know, I am just seeing this as an opportunity for growth and self-discovery." Then I would go in the bathroom and cry for 5 minutes, wipe my face, smile and walk out back out like I was the same happy, strong person everyone knew me to be. It is important to allow yourself to feel the emotions, this isn't about suppressing everything. However, after the first month or so it is time to fight back against the emotions. If She would pop in my head, I would literally say "NOPE" out loud and shift my thinking to something else. I would focus on me and loving myself and what my new goals were. If you catch yourself thinking of them, in any way…STOP, say NOPE out loud, smile (even if you have to fake it), and then think of YOU or something that makes you happy.

When I would talk to people at the beginning I would talk about the pain and the event. Then I shifted and started talking about how cool the experience was and the beauty within the pain. Instead of journaling about the pain, I journaled about what I was learning, how I was growing and what I was going to do next. I started writing this book. That alone was so therapeutic. I wrote the broken chapters while going through it and then took my own advice. It was written in past tense and so it made it feel past tense.

Watch yourself in everything you do and pivot your words, actions and choices around the positive. It seems trivial but words and thoughts are powerful, our lives are what we believe and say they are.

Here are some examples of translations from negative to positive:

Negative	Positive
He/she left me	This is a new chapter
It's been hard	It's been an opportunity for growth
I still love her	I am learning to love me
I'm too sad to do anything	I am going to say "Yes" to everything

One of the people I interviewed had gone through a horrible break up with a girl he had planned on marrying. He was devastated and went through his broken times just like the rest of us. He became anti-social and reclusive. Then one day he decided he was going to say yes to everything. One year after his breakup here is what his life has become:

"I say yes to everything now, I told myself this year is the year of YES. #yes. I put it on a t-shirt, I tag it on everything. I have been to Mexico twice. I spent two weeks in Europe, I have gone hiking in Sedona 8 times, I bought the car I wanted, I got the house I wanted, I am dating like crazy and spending really great times with really awesome people. I am just beaming positivity now. People have come to know me now in the last few months as the person if need someone to do something fun with you...I am the guy. I haven't said no to anything this year and it has felt really good. And now I am in a book!"

Make this year the year of YES! Say yes to life! Say YES to adventures and new experiences. This is your opportunity to create a whole new life for yourself, reinvent yourself.

SAY YES!

It is all about positive thinking and positive living. There are a million books on the power of positive thinking and manifesting your own destiny. The mind is a powerful thing. Napoleon Hill wrote Think and Grow Rich in 1937 and one of his most famous quotes from that book is:

"Whatever your mind can conceive and believe the mind can achieve regardless of how many times you may have failed in the past."

The book is about achieving wealth and success but the quote holds true for anything you want in life. If you can think of yourself as being happy, and truly believe you will be then you actually will be. It works in the inverse too. As Henry Ford famously said

"Whether you think you can, or you think you can't, you are right."

If you sit around thinking you'll never be happy again, you'll never find love again, that it is all your fault and all the other bullshit you tell yourself…guess what…you will be right!

"The only thing standing between you and your goal, is the bullshit story you keep telling yourself as to why you can't achieve it" – Jordan Belfort, Wolf of Wall Street

You have to tell yourself that you "got this" and that you are on your way to a better life, an exciting new chapter.

Think about it:

You don't have to ask anyone for permission to do anything

You get to buy whatever you want at the grocery store

You don't have to put the lid down

You don't have to worry about the lid not being down

You can watch whatever you want, read whatever you want

You can wear whatever you want

You can decorate or not decorate however you want

You don't have to take care of anyone else's feelings

You can DO WHATEVER YOU WANT

Relish in the little things!

Smile every time one of these hits you. Smile and enjoy the moments where you have a taste of knowing that freedom. Smile randomly for no reason. Laugh at yourself when you are being stupid. If I started to get sad I would laugh at myself and say…"are you kidding? Why would you miss someone who would hurt you and your kids? Why would you miss someone who doesn't miss you?" I would laugh and promise to love me more.

Fake it. Smile. Find laughter and joy in everything. Notice I said FIND IT, not SEE IT. Even if you don't see it. Fake it. Because one day you won't be faking it anymore.
It took me 5 months, after 8 years of complete happiness and bliss…she left me and in 5 months I was excited, happy and feeling on top of the world again…because I told myself I would be and whatever my mind can conceive and believe … it fucking achieves.

Launi Jones Sheldon– Divorce attorney 16 years, Scottsdale AZ
I always analogize it to a death that is on purpose if I get a client who it wasn't his or her choice because they are losing this person, but by the other person's choice. It makes it worse because this person chose not to be with them, this person chose to be out of their life and really take a lot of things from them.
This is what I always tell my clients when they come in. Surround yourself first with people who let you mourn the loss. No matter who wanted the split, it's a huge loss. If you

have friends who say "You are better off without him" and "he's a jerk." it minimalizes the importance of the relationship. That person wasn't always a jerk or there were times where they were nice. You don't want that relationship diminished by those comments. However, you will want these people later for the next stages. But in the beginning you have to find people who will let you mourn and cry over it.

You have to find people who understand that is big loss, and that you loved and spent a lot of time with. There is going to big uproar and change in your life and you need someone who understands that. The relationship has to be validated and the loss has to be validated. It's just like mourning a death. Your friends would never say "It's good they died" You need to go through all the processes of grieving the loss, otherwise you'll be suffering later and you are going to hold onto it and you won't know why".

You have to recognize the loss and the quicker you recognize the loss and that it is a loss and your life is going to change, it's the biggest part because after that you say "Alright I need to start planning, I need to figure out who I am without this person, I need to figure out what I like to do, you have to almost create yourself again as a single person.

People that have a plan feel like they have more control and it gives them something to focus on. Once they have a plan and they know there is going to be an end and they can start planning for it, they feel better.

Security is probably one of the biggest things people lose in a divorce, especially women who have been staying at home with their kids or didn't go out and make as big of a career. There is a lot of fear financially but the rejection is tough. Especially when there is no explanation. The responses range from people who are fed up and are done and have a peace about them, to be who are lost and frantic to people who found out their significant other was having an affair. I see it from every single different angle.

But you know there is still the devastation of the loss and each person feels that differently. If people are religious, they turn to church. If they are not religious, then its friends and family. Sometimes it's easier when there's another person there with them, kind of like a crutch and crutches aren't bad. I love when my clients have crutches when they are going through a divorce, whether it's a new boyfriend or new girlfriend, it helps them to be able to focus on what is important.

Some people can be strong and rely on themselves, and that is great but if they can't be that strong then it's good to have somebody with them. I think it makes them feel worthy and if it's after someone has rejected them they may be feeling worthless. People can feel, suicidal, depressed and friends or someone else is yes a distraction but it can also make them feel important and worthwhile and loved and liked. Those things are very important.

Sitting and wallowing makes it worse. If you have thoughts constantly that are negative you are training your brain to think negative. The bigger is when, let's say a victim of domestic violence, because they already feel pretty bad about themselves. Focusing on that and not getting help is a problem that only gets worse. Get help, get counseling. People all go through different stages. Let's say somebody comes to me and they are thinking of leaving for whatever reason. There's a book called "Love and respect" by Dr. Emerson Eggerichs, that I give to people who are having marital problems. I try to make sure that they have tried everything before they have come to me. Once they are ready, then I am a counselor and a coach.

I have had a couple people recover quickly and it was the "Fake it, until you feel it" kind of thing. They would pretend that they were fine and you knew that they weren't but eventually they were fine. Some that I have actually become very good friends with. People who just tell themselves they are good until they actually are sure of it.

Chapter 3

Own your shit

The biggest battle of your life
all comes down to strength.
Either
you heal
yourself
or you are going to crumble.
Inch by inch
day by day
till you are badass again.
You are in hell right now,
believe me
and
you can stay here
and get the shit kicked out of you
or
you can fight your way
back into the light.
You can climb out of hell.
One inch, at a time.

A revised version of Al Pacino's speech in Any Given Sunday

Chapter 3: Own your shit

Badasses own their shit. Period. Okay it's over, you hurt. Time to stand up, knock the dust off and keep going. Remember....It's not all your fault...AND...it's not all their fault either. Yes, you could have done things differently, and I am sure they could have done things differently but unless you have a time machine...

YOU CANNOT CHANGE THOSE THINGS.

NOW GET THE FUCK UP, AND DON'T EVER GIVE UP.

The sooner you acknowledge that and move on the better. Strength comes from owning OUR OWN faults, not trying to get them to acknowledge theirs. You will become a fucking genius therapist at deciding what they need to do and what they need to know about themselves but it won't do you any good.

You can only work on YOU. You can only change YOU. During the first month or so I was great at realizing what I needed to do. I knew all my flaws and everywhere I went wrong. I apologized a million times and I went to therapy, got outside, ran, meditated, journaled. All the things I am telling you to do. But guess where I went wrong...I did it for HER, not me. I would tell her all my epiphanies, I would show her how I had changed and what I was doing. I acknowledged all of my faults and how I knew I could be better.

Guess what she did. She acknowledged all my faults too, she jumped right on board with hating me and seeing the worst in me. We both were all about MY flaws. It didn't do me any good. First, it fucked up her path of self-acknowledging and self-growth because if we both agreed that it was me then why would she need to look within herself? And no wonder she couldn't respect me, I wasn't respecting myself.

Two, although all the change was good and I was moving in the right direction it would never be pure or as good as it could be if I wasn't doing it for myself. It turned from introspection to self-hatred as we both blamed me.

There is a difference
between being introspective and self-loathing.
Don't get them confused.

It wasn't until I remembered that I am a fucking badass. I crush life. I am a good person who always put others first. I am full of life and love and ideas and adventures. I dream big,

I love big and I live big. I am not perfect, but I am badass and I am proud of who I am. I was getting texts, emails and calls from so many people who were telling me the impact I had on their lives and how much they valued me. Some people that I had only had a few encounters with…if these people could see value in me, why shouldn't I? And if she can't….FUCK HER and FUCK THEM if they don't love YOU… why would you want to force them to? Are you that pathetic that you think you are only worth begging for their love? No. You aren't pathetic and they aren't worth your tears, your pain or your begging. You don't need to hate them either. You need to NOTHING them. Let them go, forget them and turn your love to yourself.

Also, after the first few weeks nobody wants to hear you bitch and complain anymore. The one thing I am proud of during this whole ordeal was not bad mouthing Her to anyone else. She was telling people her side of the story, that wasn't necessarily untrue but conveniently left out the entire half of the event that makes me NOT look like a psycho and gives her 50% of the blame. I fought back and told my side of the story to a couple people we shared in common. Our situation was 24 hours of mistakes on both parts and neither of was free from blame. However, she kept repeating my faults without acknowledging her own. I kept repeating my faults without acknowledging her responsibility. That was fun. I held onto this bullshit for way too long. Who cares what anyone thinks about you or your relationship.

The good news is that now, from a bird's eye view...I am glad I am me because it is only through recognizing where I am, can I see where I need to go. I walked through hell, survived, found my true self and wrote a book that is now helping you. That is pretty badass.

As a matter of fact, did you know that when you speak negatively about others that people tend to associate those characteristics with you? If you keep repeating what a piece of shit your ex is, they will start to think that you are indeed that piece of shit. Tell yourself that IT DOES NOT MATTER what anyone on their side thinks. It doesn't matter what they think or say. Say out loud every time your brain goes crazy: IT DOESN'T MATTER.

Instead, let them go. I pretended like she died. It helped.

That way there are no hard feelings. It's not like someone can help that they died. I can't be mad at her for dying.

Right now imagine your ex as though they are no longer on the planet. Mourn their absence. Have a wake and let them go.

And

Never speak ill of the dead.

Chapter 4

The New Love of Your Life

"If you can't love yourself, how the hell are you gonna love anyone else" – Rupaul

Chapter 4: The new love of your life

You have heard it a million times in a million ways...

"Love yourself"

"Love thyself"

"You have to Mr. Right to find Mrs. Right"

"Be your own best friend"

"To thine own self be true"

Blah. Blah. Blah.

People hand these out like candy, because they don't always know what else to say. It depends on the day but my reactions to clichés like these vary widely. On a good day I would say "Absolutely, I love me and I know that it starts with me!"

On a bad day I would probably say "Go fuck yourself, I want someone else to hold and love me for me"

The truth is; in life no one will ever fully love you the way YOU can love you. NOONE.

There is something powerful that happens when you develop a love affair with yourself. One of the coolest books that I read during this time, that had a big impact on me, was Kamal Ravikant's "Love Yourself – Like Your Life Depends on it." It is the shortest book I have ever read and the cheapest, but I guess good things come in small packages. Kamal doesn't say anything ground breaking, it is simply about loving yourself. However, it is the way he says it and there is beauty in the simplicity of how he writes. For some reason this book hit home with me. I started saying to myself all day "I love myself" and it really worked. I also would think of how I would treat myself if I was in love with myself and started doing those things.

As I was running one morning I just kept repeating "I love myself" and then I started saying what I loved about myself. After a while I realized I was smiling as I was running. I got back and wrote this in my journal:

I love my heart for others. That I am a giver and I get my feeling of importance from helping others.

I love my drive and ambition. That I never give up and I always accomplish everything I set out to do.

I love that I am such a good mom and I have given the girls such a great life

I love that I adopted the boys and we love each other so much

I love my body. It's beautiful. I have beautiful everything. I love my legs, toes, face, teeth, smile, eyes, hands, butt. I love me.

I am going to give me whatever I want. I am going to spoil me. Take me places and give myself a dream life. I am going to take care of me and love me.

I am going to take care of my health, my happiness, my finances and my heart.

I love myself.

I am going to embrace life and do whatever I want!

I am a good person who deserves all the love, and there is nobody better than me to give it to me.

When I wrote the part about giving myself whatever I wanted I felt giddy inside. I had always only focused on whatever anyone else needed and put myself last, but it was so exciting to think of loving ME and putting ME first. Also, I am god damn romantic so I knew I could wine and dine the shit out of myself. I have always wanted to be with someone like me who gives so much love, would never say a bad thing to me and would spoil me. I get to be my very own dream girl.

You can be your own dream person! Let's start with, what you love about yourself:

Mentally:

Physically:

Relationally:

Anything else:

What would you do for yourself if you were dating and actively loving YOU:

There will never be anyone who knows you as well as you know yourself. There will never be anyone whose love is as impactful as the love you can give yourself. If you learn how to love yourself the way you should be loved, then you will be less likely to settle for anyone who isn't willing to love you the same.

I always spoiled my wife, put her above anyone else, loved her with every ounce of my being...but I forgot about me. Now I love myself the way I used to love Her and it feels really great. Think about how much love you gave them, what you did for them, now imagine doing all of that for yourself.

Give yourself the live you deserve. Say it with me "I LOVE MYSELF"

***Daily exercise: Look in the mirror and say "I love you" and tell yourself what is great about yourself. It's fucking weird and uncomfortable at first, then it feels nice.

Anonymous Male – 32 years old
There was this moment in late 2014 where our relationship was kind of on the rock already and I was offered a position in Chicago and I wasn't sure if I wanted her to come with me yet. I knew that if I invited her to come it would be moving in

together and making a big step in the direction of making a serious run at things. I was unsure if I wanted that and she was obviously very hurt and devastated by my inability to choose a side and ability to give her any kind of clear path to our future.

She started seeing someone else behind my back and it turns out that it lasted probably three or four months. I later found out the hard way she was cheating on me and finding out was probably one of the most devastating hits I have taken in my life. I had this crazy realization that I really did need her in my life, I felt shameful and embarrassed that I had been so indecisive and I wanted to make things right even though she cheated on me, I tried to find a way to take some ownership as well because I didn't give her the answers that she needed. Deep down inside, as hurt as I was, I couldn't really blame her.

I made a really strong push for her to give us another chance and for me to be very concise and clear about what I wanted. I wanted her to move to Chicago with me and I wanted her to be the biggest part of my life. I was finally ready to really commit and she was happy because that is what she wanted all along. I was happy too because I felt in love with somebody for the first time in years, I finally felt this sense of surrender to a relationship and I finally felt like I had a partner.

She wasn't quite living in Chicago yet, as she was getting ready for the move and her company was preparing to transfer her. But things were for a couple months, looking really good. I flew her to meet my family. They loved her, I loved her. I was in the process of ring shopping. I wanted to do everything, I wanted to make it right and make it romantic. I wanted her to land in Chicago and have this glorious, ceremonial "welcome to my life," I was going to fly her parents in and surprise her with asking her to marry me.

Then somewhere along the line, she was on a trip and I found out through a series of photos on social media that she went to lunch with this guy that I didn't really know. I asked her about it and she denied it. I showed her the photo, and she admitted to it apologized and said she was nervous to tell me because he was just a friend and she didn't want me to over react because there was nothing romantic happening.

That led to me spending the next two months being extremely jealous and nervous and doubtful of everything she was doing. I found myself going through her phone, asking her questions of where she was every single day. It ended up being really nasty. I turned into the kind of man that I personally don't like. I turned into the kind of man where I always tell the women in my life not to date. I was turning into that guy because I couldn't trust her anymore. I told her if she would just be honest with me, while it might hurt at first, it would be better.

Over the course of the next month I found things her phone that were very suspect, very flirtatious, texts with other guys and I also found out that the night after she moved in with me in Chicago that her relationship with the guy she cheated on me with never really ended. They will still in communication, they were still seeing each other. She had his name in her phone as a female so I wouldn't catch on. That went on for a little while, I finally found out and I was devastated. I lost my cool, I yelled at her. I kicked her out of my apartment. I couldn't breathe I couldn't see straight. She swore nothing was going on she swore she loved me, she swore she wanted to spend the rest of her life with me. I couldn't understand how you could tell someone you love them and still see someone else behind their back. She wanted to stay and make things work but I found myself to be angrier than I have ever been in my whole life. I kicked her out and she moved her stuff into storage.

 She lived with a friend of hers in Chicago that she knew from her college days. I was alone, I was upset, I lived in an apartment that I couldn't afford and I was really devastated. I found myself sleeping for weeks on end, crying every single day, not being able to smile. Even the little things that usually made me happy like hanging out with my friends. I even tried to make it work even after that. I think that is the part that upsets me the most, even after all of that I was still the one that still was trying. The part the hurt the most wasn't that I got cheated on but that I lost my self-respect because the advice I would give all my friends would be "Hey, what the fuck is wrong with you? That girl just cheated on you. Kick her to the curb don't ever talk to her again. Don't ever put yourself in a situation where you let someone disrespect you like that" and I ended up being the one who was disrespected and I even saw myself going back for seconds, thirds and fourths because I missed her and loved her so much. She ended up moving away from Chicago. I stayed.

To get through the darkest times I relied on my family. They recognized that I was going through a very rough time. I have two amazing sisters and they flew from across the country to come spend some time with their brother, they made sure that I felt loved and secure. I probably could not have done it without them because there were definitely suicidal thoughts. I needed my family to help me get through that. I had to surround myself with positivity. I found that working really hard actually ended up being healthy. I found that volunteering was good. I helped the homeless by spending time in homeless shelters. I gave a lot of money to the homeless organization. The feeling of helping others who needed it more than me was very rewarding and made me feel like although I am going through a severe heartache, there are people out there that are freezing in the cold without a place to sleep. Volunteering my time with people who didn't have much, was really great. Doing those things made me realize that my problems aren't as severe as other people's.

Its been a little over two years since we were together and I still don't feel whole. What I do to constantly remind myself is tell myself all the good things about myself and own the good things that are within me, instead of telling myself the wrong things.

I say yes to everything now, I told myself this year is the year of YES. #yes. I put it on a t-shirt, I tag it on everything. I have been to Mexico twice. I spent two weeks in Europe, I have gone hiking in Sedona 8 times, I bought the car I wanted, I got the house I wanted, I am dating like crazy and spending really great times with really awesome people. I am just beaming positivity now. People have come to know me now in the last few months as the person if need someone to do something fun with you...I am the guy. I haven't said no to anything this year and it has felt really good. And now I am in a book!

Chapter 5

Get your Bad ASS outside

When you bring your attention to a stone, a tree or an animal, something of its essence transmits itself to you. You can sense how still it is and in doing so the same stillness rises within you. You can sense how deeply it rests in being, completely one with what it is and where it is, in realizing this, you too come to a place or rest deep within yourself. ~ Author unknown

Chapter 5: Get your badass outside

Badasses are not couch potatoes. I too love a good Harry Potter marathon when it's raining but if you find yourself watching TV every night, you need to get your priorities straight. Growth does not happen whilst staring at the TV or your phone. You know the saying that "it takes less brain power to watch TV than to stare at a blank wall"? I'm not sure how accurate that is but it makes a lot of fucking sense. That is why TV feels so good, that's why you can mindlessly scroll through Facebook for hours. Because for once you don't have to think.

Yet, when I meditate I stare at a blank wall and my mind goes crazy. I think a million things, pivot, breathe, focus, relax, think, relax, breathe…ARRRGGHH.

Get outside. Even right now, if you are laying in bed get your ass up and go outside and read. Nature is healing.

Okay I live in Arizona and in the summer you couldn't pay me to be outside. If you are in Chicago and it's winter, probably the same. But sit by a window and turn off the TV, put your phone in a drawer. Turn the music off. Let nature come in through the window. Or bundle up and get your damn snow shoes on. In Arizona, get in the pool, in the shade for the love of god. But get outside and away from technology.

We are addicted to technology and it feels good to stare at it, it eases our suffering and calms our brains. It also impedes our growth and stifles self-reflection. Being in nature can help stop negative, obsessive thoughts because you are more at peace and distracted visually. Getting outside can also help with weight loss and fitness. Think REVENGE BODY! There really is no better diet than heartbreak. I lost 17lbs in 5 weeks. Yes, I wasn't eating a lot but I was also running. I love running because I feel great afterwards from the boost of endorphins but during I just listen to positive motivational videos and train my brain to be disciplined.

Aside from running, there is hiking, biking, swimming, walking...the list goes on. If you aren't an "outdoor" person, it is probably because you have not tried it. I wasn't a camping person before this. I was a total snob. My idea of camping was when we stayed at a shitty hotel on our layover to fly to a little tropical island before our stay at the W. Yet, as soon as she left I bought camping gear and went camping for the first time in forever. Being outside felt so good.

If you truly want to be a badass and have a badass life, it won't be found in front of your phone or the TV. We spend so much time looking at other people's lives that we forget to live our own. UNPLUG. Even if it is just a little bit at first, do an hour of quiet time. Read a few chapters of a great book outside on a chair. Walk to the store instead of driving. Hike instead of shopping. Picnic instead of going to a restaurant. But get outside, because badassery is never found on a couch.

Chapter 6

Revenge Life

The best revenge is to show them your life is getting better after they are gone.

Chapter 6: Revenge Life

They hurt you, crushed you and let you walk through hell....meanwhile....you have spent the last few days, weeks, months crying over them. You have wasted your precious time giving them energy that they don't deserve.

The best revenge is to be happy, accomplish your goals, look amazing and become the best version of yourself. Imagine if you ran into your ex. How you would want to look? What would you like to be able to say you have accomplished?

By month 5 I had hit my goal weight, was exercising every day, wrote a book, got a promotion at work, had made new friends and done things I had never done before...like go to Mexico for 4 days, Long beach pride, see fireflies for the first time with some cool person I randomly met online and St. Louis pride with a new friend.

Time to do a self-inventory. Let's take a look at your life and see where you can improve and what goals you need to set and accomplish. It is absolutely crucial that you are very specific about what you want to accomplish. Your goals need to have a timeline and be quantifiable to achieve the best results. Example, instead of saying "I want to be in shape" say "I want to be at 125lbs by July 30th and I want to have worked out 3 times a week so that my butt is firm and my arms no longer wobble". SPECIFIC! If you aren't specific, with quantifiable goals, it leaves too much to interpretation and chance. Giving yourself set goals give you something to shoot for in your 3 month, 6 month and 1 year plans.

Where do you rate in each area on a scale of 1 -10 1 being nowhere close to where you want to be and 10 being you couldn't be any better.

Physically: 1 2 3 4 5 6 7 8 9 10

Are you in the best shape you can be? If not, what would you change?

Are you healthy and happy physically?

Is there anything you have always wanted to change or improve about your appearance?

Why haven't you done it in the past? How can you do it now?

Write a 3 month, 6 month and 1 year plan to accomplish your ideal physical health.

Mentally: 1 2 3 4 5 6 7 8 9 10

Other than the break up, what are your biggest stresses in life right now?

What is your current stress management approach? Is it working?

Name three things that make you happiest?

How often do you do those things?

Write a 3 month, 6 month and 1 year plan to achieve your ideal mental health:

Financially: 1 2 3 4 5 6 7 8 9 10

What is your ideal financial health profile?

What holds you back from being at your ideal financial state?

Where do you spend money that you shouldn't?

How much money do you have saved?

Write out a 3 month, 6 month and 1 year plan to achieve your ideal financial health:

Other:

What has been on your bucket list for awhile that you keep putting off?

Set a plan to accomplish those things:
Step 1:

Step 2:

Step 3:

I commit to the following DAILY activities that will get me closer to my goals:

Now think about the person who you will meet in the future, your ideal partner. Once again it is crucial that you are VERY specific. These things have a way of manifesting themselves so if you say you want them to own a "house" and you aren't specific, they may own a run down house in a bad neighborhood. Say I would like my future partner to "Own a nice house, in a specific part of town, with a backyard and nice pool" Or you can be even more specific. You will be surprised at what will come to you if you ask for it.

What is ideal future relationship?

What do they look like, act like?

How do they treat you?

What does their financial profile look like?

Where do they live?

What else?

Okay now you have written out your ideal life. You need a big calendar that you can use to track your progress to your goals. Hang it somewhere that you will pass frequently and get in the habit of marking it every day around the same time. I even put my mood on the with emoji faces. I know what days I am happy and what days I am sad, then I can look back and see what contributed to those feelings.

You don't have to accomplish it all at once or even this year. All you have to do to be badass is NEVER GIVE UP and do something little every single day to bring you closer to your goals. If it's going for a walk instead of a run. Stretching instead of going to the gym. Turning the TV off and reading one single chapter. Eat half a burrito instead of the whole thing. Pay off half a credit card and cut it up so you at least don't spend anymore. Have one glass of wine instead of two. Call a friend and catch up for 20 minutes. Put $10 in your savings even if you can't put that $100 you wanted to.

All the little things add up towards your progress.

DO SOMETHING EVERY SINGLE DAY TO MOVE YOU CLOSER TO YOUR GOALS.

Chapter 7

Backsliding

I see you.

I see you grinding another day, battered and exhausted refusing to stop.

I see your fists swollen and split knuckled: dripping with the quit you beat to the ground.

I see you, your tired eyes bloodshot from blinking against the grains of you'll never be enough, that are swirling sandstorms across your vision.

I see you, the fight in you, and it is ferocious.

I see you, the heart of you, and it is breathtaking.

I see you, the soul of you, and it is magnificent.

I see you.

All of you.

And you are fucking beautiful.

- N. Lyons

Chapter 7: Backsliding

Watersliding, slipsliding, sledsliding...all fun. Not to be confused with backsliding which is not fucking fun. You will be going along, all happy go lucky. Thinking you made it through and you are a badass and life is great, then WHAM some bullshit hits you in the fucking face.

It was month three and I was on top of the world. I was feeling great and had adhered to my two months and done rule, then I had been in St. Louis for three weeks for work and just got back home. The apartment was still a cave, our bed was still empty and a sadness came over me. It wasn't so bad until I completely went full idiot and text Her. Begging her to just talk to me, oh and she talked to me. Turns out the reason why she was so fucking cold and it was so easy for her overnight was because she was dating a girl I used to date. They were now living together and had been for the past month. She left me for someone else and two months later, she was in a relationship and living with one of my ex's. Everything came spiraling down and pieces of the puzzle came slamming together as I realized that fateful night before the break up when she had sent me a text photo of this "friend" of ours and then stopped texting me, she had fallen for her. I didn't even think of it at the time. She was MY forever girl, so why would she fall for someone else? Then the times she was texting in the bedroom when I was at work and our daughter walked in and She quickly put her phone away and seemed so guilty, she was texting this other girl. This heartless bitch let me writhe in pain for months, wracking my brain as to what the fuck happened to us. I couldn't figure out for the life of me what had gone wrong, how did we go from perfect to nothing? I blamed myself, I wanted to die... meanwhile she was with someone else. She left our kids, she left me and she was living with someone else. Numerous people had asked me "Is it someone else?" and I said no... but honestly it was the only thing that would have made sense. Someone even said "It's always someone else, even if you don't think it is." I didn't think it was. It was.

Holy mother of god, does that shit hurt. The best analogy about backsliding I can think of is; it is like running a marathon with no training and feeling like you are going to die but surviving and just when you get to sit down take a rest and breathe, someone makes you run a marathon again. You are exhausted from pushing through the first time, you are disheartened because you really thought you were feeling good again and you are heartbroken all over again.

There's an emptiness to this stage, at least there was for me. It's all the pain from the first weeks but there's a missing energy, almost like your soul and heart have given up so long ago that they don't have fight left in them, so they just try to hold you above the darkness without having the strength to crawl out. This one is almost harder than the first time because this time you don't have all the strong emotions and adrenaline. This time it just is. You also most likely have depleted the energy of your support group at this point and they give you a less astounding support response. They watched you overcome it the last time and they know you can do it again, but they don't realize it's almost square one for you.

Okay, so it happened you backslid. The early chapters won't help AS MUCH. They may still help but the effects are lessened because you already know all of that. Now is the time you need the friends who I told you to avoid. Now you need the friends who will tell you that They are a piece of shit and They don't deserve you. You need friends who don't coddle you but tell you to "STOP FEELING SORRY FOR YOURSELF AND GET THE FUCK UP"

You also need to adopt the NOPE technique we used before. If you find yourself thinking about it, literally say NOPE outloud and pivot your thinking away. NOPE you aren't going to think about it. NOPE.

You have to go back to saying "I love myself" "I love myself" OVER AND OVER.

Drown out the bullshit your brain is handing you. Your brain is a fucking asshole and cannot be trusted. It is lying to you constantly and holding you prisoner. I hate how my brain just keeps replaying shit that I don't want to see or think about. I hate it.

God damn it if we can overcome it the first time we can overcome it this time. It happened and now we have to do it again, and truth be told, it may not be the last time. But for every time we get up and run that marathon again we are getting stronger, better and more resilient.

This is heartbreak boot camp and it sucks, and you are tired and you have no idea what even makes it worth it anymore. This where motivational videos help. There are a ton on YouTube and I would just play them one after another. Just pumping my brain full of strong words and positivity.

I know you can't feel it right now but you just felt happy not too long ago.
Nothing has changed, you are on the right path.
You can do this.
If it takes a dozen times, you are strong and you can do this.
They can't hold you down anymore and you aren't going to beg someone to love you because you are worth more than that.
Their choices are theirs, and your choices are yours. You have to make the choice AGAIN, and maybe again, but you will.

Stand up, say NOPE and try again.

Final words:

This journey is yours and yours alone. No-one can judge the time it takes for you to heal or the path you travel. The road to being badass is far beyond the reach of anyone who has hurt you. This is about you. My heart hurts for the woman I was when I went through this, she was so alone and in pain. But she grew and is she is a badass and I love her. I am putting all my love and energy into myself and my family and life has never been better. Instead of making someone else's dreams come true, I am making all my own dreams come true and it's glorious.

As Tupac once said:
"You can't force them to love you or want you, but one day you'll make them realize what they lost"

And when they do, you won't want them anymore.

Sources:

Chodron, Pema. *When Things Fall Apart: Heart Advice for Difficult Times (20th Anniversary Edition)*. Shambhala Publications Inc, 2016.

Sark. *Succulent wild woman: dancing with your wonder-Full self!* Simon & Schuster, 1997.

Sandberg, Sheryl, and Adam Grant. *Option B: facing adversity, building resilience, and finding joy*. WH Allen, en imprint of Ebury Publishing, 2017.

Gilbert, Elizabeth. *Eat, Pray, Love*. Bloomsbury Publishing Ltd., 2016.

Robbins, Mel. *The 5 second rule: transform your life, work, and confidence with everyday courage*. Savio Republic, 2017.

HILL, NAPOLEON. *THINK AND GROW RICH*. CRESTLINE BOOKS, 2017.

Ravikant, Kamal. *Love yourself like your life depends on it.* CreateSpace, 2012.

173

Printed in Great Britain
by Amazon